Maria Barker 9-24-97

REVELATION
Through
First Century
Glasses

W.B. WEST JR.

REVELATION

Through First Century Glasses

EDITED WITH INTRODUCTION BY

BOB PRICHARD

Gospel Advocate Company
1006 Elm Hill Pike
Nashville, Tennessee 37210

All Scripture quotations are from the King James Version.

Published by Gospel Advocate Co.
1006 Elm Hill Pike
Nashville, TN 37210
e-mail: gospeladv@aol.com

ISBN 0-89225-465-3

TABLE OF CONTENTS

THE SEVEN CHURCHES OF ASIA

Dr. West
As I Knew Him

Fresh out of the Air Force and just beginning to understand what preparation for preaching the gospel meant, I began studies at the Harding University Graduate School of Religion in 1976. "Revelation" under Dr. W.B. West Jr. was one of the courses I signed up for that fall. I did not know him or his work then because I did not "grow up in the church." Dr. West had already retired from the deanship but was still teaching. To most of us students he seemed quite old, although by his standards he was still young. That first semester he invited E.H. Ijams, then in his 90s, to speak to the class so that we could get the perspective of an "older preacher."

Very quickly I learned that Dr. West was a different kind of teacher. He had a genuine love for his students that went beyond any I had ever seen before in a graduate school teacher. It was not long until I went to him for his sage advice on several pressing problems, and he always had time for me. My wife Sharon began doing secretarial work for him, and as we got to know him, we loved him more and more. We invited him to our home to eat with us and learned what a gracious guest he was. Although he had the justly earned reputation of loving all the students, we knew that he had a special interest in us. Visiting with Dr. West often involved moving books, but as a fellow book lover, I really could appreciate his vast library. We could always talk books (or move them).

With graduation, our relationship changed somewhat, but we had already become friends, and he would always be my wisest advisor and mentor. Trips to Memphis for lectureships and activities were never complete without a visit to Dr. West. I always set aside at least one afternoon to visit with him (and move books). His concern for my family continued. After an eloquent lesson at the Spiritual Sword Lectureship, brethren crowded around him. We exchanged general pleasantries as almost everyone else did, and he asked how we were doing. Then, when the crowd thinned out, he said, "And now, how are you *really* doing?" He had a genuine concern for my family, my congregations and me.

After he moved to Montgomery, Alabama, to teach, he gave his lecture series near Elba, Alabama, where we were then living. He made a point of praising me from the pulpit in such glowing terms that he made me truly feel like royalty. We continued to visit together, and when the opportunity arose, we invited him to come to Elba to speak on Revelation. It was there that we were able to introduce him, now a widower, to Sharon's mother, who also was widowed. Their acquaintance resulted in marriage in 1987 and made me his son-in-law, although he had treated me like a son for years. I began the ceremony saying, "It is a double honor for me to assist in this marriage of two people for whom I have the utmost love and respect. Each has honored me by loving me and treating me as a son." The marriage allowed us to share much more, although never enough, time together. Holidays, lectureships, birthdays and vacations were precious because of the time we shared.

Dr. West loved the church, and whenever we had opportunity we discussed the cause of Christ. Each evening the family would gather for prayer and a devotional reading, usually from Revelation. He always called on me to read the Scripture and lead the prayer. I believe that he chose to do this to honor me. It was always a sad moment when we had to leave after those visits. At his request, we would join hands and sing "Blest Be the Tie That Binds."

> Blest be the tie that binds
> Our hearts in Christian love,
> The fellowship of kindred minds,
> Is like to that above.
>
> Before our Father's throne,
> We pour our ardent prayers,

Our fears, our hopes, our aims are one,
Our comforts and our cares.

We share our mutual woes,
Our mutual burdens bear,
And often for each other flows
The sympathizing tear.

When we asunder part,
It gives us inward pain,
But we shall still be joined in heart,
And hope to meet again.

The sentiment of that hymn well-describes the W.B. West I knew. His ability to get along with the brethren wherever and whenever was truly amazing. Brethren everywhere loved him because they could see in his life that he truly was bound in Christian love to them and that the heaven he preached about so often as a home for all was real. He grieved at the burdens brethren bore, and he rejoiced in the triumphs of the faith. He certainly felt that inward pain when we parted, but he knew that God's children would meet again.

He taught me much about respect through his example. He had the same kind greeting for the waitress or the janitor as he did for the college president. He was a people person to the core. He frequently solicited my judgment on issues and questions, not because he did not know what to do but because he was genuinely interested in what I thought. He counted me as his equal, although I did not feel that way. On more than one occasion he personally awarded me an honorary "doctorate."

He was also a giving person. He shared what he had with others in need. Over the last few years he gave me several good books because he knew that they would help me to teach and reach out to others. My continued education was of special interest to him, and he offered all the help and encouragement that he could give. When he taught on the writings of the apostle John, he would often speak of the aged apostle being brought into the assembly at Ephesus, where the brethren would ask him, "Brother John, is there any word of admonition you would like to give us?" His reply was, "My little children, love one another." They then said, "Brother John, is there anything else you want to tell us?" His reply was, "No, if you will love one another, that will be enough." Dr. West taught me to love the brethren. His love was apparent to all, and his brethren returned his love.

Heaven was one of his favorite subjects. That was the topic of his Wednesday night sermon in that fortuitous meeting in Elba. I was with him that morning shortly after he received word that his only sister had died. While sorrow weighed heavily on his heart, he preached the most heartfelt sermon on heaven I have ever heard. As he spoke of the beauty of heaven, I knew that he was not just speaking about a subject he had an interest in, but he was speaking with all the conviction he could bring concerning a home he longed for. He could say, like Paul, "I am in a strait betwixt two, having a desire to depart, and to be with Christ; which is far better: nevertheless to abide in the flesh *is* more needful for you" (Philippians 1:23-24). He set the example for me of being prepared for heaven but continuing to serve the Lord here. He spoke to me of spending eternity in the heavenly library, studying and serving the Lord. He expected to serve God in eternity the same way he had in life.

He wanted us to work together on his commentary on Revelation. Often he would say, "I wish we lived closer, Bob, so that we could work together." It disturbed him that he was unable to complete his commentary, but as Dr. Bill Flatt, Dean of Harding University Graduate School of Religion, pointed out at his funeral, he wrote his commentary in the hearts of his students. Surely this is what Paul wanted Timothy to do when he admonished, "The things that thou hast heard of me among many witnesses, the same commit thou to faithful men, who shall be able to teach others also" (2 Timothy 2:2).

Since Dr. West was unable to complete the publication of his lectures on Revelation, I have had the privilege of compiling and editing his lectures for publication. We hope to follow this volume with one containing several of his other sermons, and a commentary from his notes is under way. As I edited his lectures, I saw his unmatched classical eloquence combined with common sense and clarity. Although he was conversant with the greatest minds of the ages, his lectures were never "ivory tower dissertations." His lessons on topics such as "The Mark of the Beast," "The Battle of Armageddon," and "Heaven, Will We Know Each Other There?" touch the heart with moving illustrations and applications. While few were willing to accept fully his frequent assertion that "the book of Revelation is the easiest book in the Bible to understand," he nonetheless brought its message to life in his sermons. Ralph Waldo Emerson said, "There is no eloquence without a man behind it." All who heard Dr. West knew what kind of man was behind his eloquence.

PREFACE

More than 30 years ago the author of the lectures in this book became interested in a serious study of the book of Revelation and it continued through the intervening years. Throughout these years he has taught the book in undergraduate and graduate classrooms in Christian colleges and universities. He has also spoken on the book in scores of churches in the United States and abroad. He has planned for a number of years an advanced commentary on the book of Revelation, but other work prevented that project. On two recent occasions, his good friend C. Philip Slate, Dean of the Graduate School of Religion of Harding University in Memphis, Tennessee, suggested that he publish a selection of his lectures as he had delivered them orally in schools and churches. These lectures form this present book.

W.B.West Jr.
April 28, 1991

Editor's note: Dr. West wrote this before his death in anticipation of the publication of his lectures.

The book of Revelation is a very great and important book. All the preceding 65 books of the Bible look forward to it. It presents the culmination of all the purposes of God for mankind. It is the finale of all the written revelation of God to man, the crowning book of the Bible, portraying Paradise lost in the morning of time and regained in the Saturday evening of time. The Tree of Life, forbidden to Adam and Eve, will grow in heaven on both sides of the river of the water of life "clear as crystal, proceeding out of the throne of God and of the Lamb" (Revelation 22:1). The book of Revelation, more than any other book of the Bible, presents heaven with all of its beauties and joys throughout all eternity, and it also portrays hell as a place of eternal punishment in contrast to heaven. As no other book of the Bible, it teaches the triumph of the Kingdom of God. Its key verse is, "The kingdoms of this world are become *the kingdoms* of our Lord, and of his Christ; and he shall reign for ever and ever" (Revelation 11:15).

Words cannot adequately express the greatness and importance of the book of Revelation. Through the centuries different parts of it have been the topic of conversation by millions of people. Men have preached many thousands of sermons and sung hundreds of songs based upon it. It has made heaven real to multitudes. The word "heaven" is on thousands of inscriptions in mausoleums and on many millions of tombstones. Parts of the book have been the last words of devoted Christians as they have exchanged time for eternity and earth for heaven. Although it is encouraging that millions of people across the centuries have loved, read and studied Revelation, it is discouraging that many thousands of people have neglected, abused and misused it.

Some years ago, I preached one Sunday for the church of Christ in a small American city, attending the adult Bible class before the worship service. Near the end of the class, the teacher commented, "We are finishing this morning Third John and shall study the book of Jude next Sunday. What shall we study after we have finished Jude?" There was an immediate and unanimous response from the class, "Anything but the book of Revelation. We don't know anything about it, and we do not believe that you do. Let us turn back again to the book of Matthew."

I later learned that the class had turned back to Matthew, as it had done a number of times before. This was regrettable, not that they began a study of Matthew, but that they completely neglected the book of Revelation. In essence, what occurred in that class has happened in multiplied thousands of churches of Christ and in other religious groups across the world times without number. This is all the more regrettable inasmuch as the book of Revelation is the only book of the Bible that promises a blessing to the reader and to the one who hears and keeps the "things which are written therein" (Revelation 1:3). This does not exclude blessings gained from reading, hearing and obeying the teachings of all the books of the Bible, but it is a statement showing, in part, the significance of Revelation.

It does appear that the study of the book of Revelation is the most neglected of all the books of the Bible. There are at least two reasons for this neglect: (1) the misuse and abuse of its study, and (2) the incomplete understanding of the nature of the book. There is probably no book of the Bible as abused and misused in its study, interpretation and application as the book of Revelation. Many would-be students of the book become discouraged when they go to the commentaries on Revelation and find that seldom do two commentators agree as to the meaning of a passage. There are so many different interpretations of a passage that the inquiring student wonders if the commentators are commenting on the same passage in the same book. Often a commentator, or someone else, will go to a passage to prove what he or she already believes and not to learn what the passage teaches. Some would-be students move John out of Revelation and move in themselves. The technical term for this is eisegesis, as opposed to exegesis, which is to learn what the passage teaches and not what the "eisegete" wants it to teach. In reality, the eisegetical commentator has moved out John and moved himself in. The important thing to know is, "What do John and the text say?"

The best way to study the book of Revelation is through "first-century glasses," a phrase the writer of this book coined decades ago. The late C.H. Dodd of Cambridge University, a New Testament scholar of world renown, stated that in essence the first responsibility of a student, teacher or preacher of the New Testament is to sit with the author of any New Testament passage to learn what he had in mind and then to sit with those to whom he wrote and see what they understood the author to say. This is the bottom line in studying and teaching the book of Revelation.

In 1964, I taught an extension course in Aylesbury, England, for the Harding Graduate School of Religion. In the opening lecture, I stated to the students, "I do not ask you to agree with my understanding of the book of Revelation or any part of it, but I am requesting that you study any part or the whole of it through first-century glasses." When we finished the course, the students gave me a party of appreciation, in typical British fashion, with the gift of a pair of glasses that looked as if they were from the first century of our era! They found these glasses in an Oxford antique shop. After my return to the states, information came to me that the students in that course were continuing to study Revelation though "first-century glasses." I repeat, this is the best way to study the book of Revelation if you wish to understand it.

Let us now begin to learn how to study through "first-century glasses." In spirit, let us go from where we are across land and sea to the Roman Empire of the first and second centuries A.D., especially to the region of Asia Minor. Here we find the churches that were the primary and immediate audience for the book of Revelation. These were the churches in Ephesus, Smyrna, Pergamum, Thyatira, Sardis, Philadelphia and Laodicea (Revelation 1:11). The Roman Empire was the largest, the most powerful and the richest empire the world had ever known. The Romans boasted that the Roman Eagles (standards representing the Roman armies) never turned backward and that the Empire would be eternal with all roads leading to or from Rome.

Although Rome was a mighty empire, it was a very divided one. Many attempted to unite it, but none was successful until Rome declared the empire to be divine and its emperor also divine, being Lord and God. All would worship the emperor and thus would also declare the empire over which he ruled to be divine. Only the Jews were exempt from emperor worship. The Romans recognized the Jews as a monotheistic people of long standing, who were very important to the welfare of the Roman world.

For the Christians, the situation was different. By this time, the Romans considered them atheists because they refused to worship the Greek and Roman gods and goddesses, and the Roman emperor and empire. The Romans judged them to be a "third race" because their way of life was far different from the Greeks and Romans and other polytheistic people of the Greco-Roman world. Romans 1:28-32 paints a dark picture of the sins of the pagans in the Roman world. "And even as they did not like to retain God *in their* knowledge, God gave them over to a reprobate mind, to do those things which are not convenient; being filled with all unrighteousness, fornication, wickedness, covetousness, maliciousness; full of envy, murder, debate, deceit, malignity; whisperers, backbiters, haters of God, despiteful, proud, boasters, inventors of evil things, disobedient to parents, without understanding, covenant-breakers, without natural affection, implacable, unmerciful: who knowing the judgment of God, that they which commit such things are worthy of death, not only do the same, but have pleasure in them that do them." There were women in that world who could count the number of their years by the number of husbands that they had had.

War between the church and the Empire began as a local expression in Rome with the persecution of the Christians by the Emperor Nero after the burning of Rome in A.D. 64. Nero used the Christians as a scapegoat to turn away accusations that he had burned Rome himself. That persecution was local. In the ninth decade of the first century, however, Domitian, whom many considered to be Nero reincarnated, began another. While the persecution of Nero was local, that of Domitian was more far-reaching.

For the first time in the history of the Roman Empire, the emperor of the Roman world demanded that all his subjects (except the Jews) worship him as Lord and God and the Roman Empire as divine. This was in the person of Flavius Domitianus (Domitian), the son of Emperor Vespasian and the brother of Emperor Titus. He especially commanded and demanded that Christians so worship. When they failed, he burned them at the stake or threw them to the lions. Some, such as John the apostle, had the lesser punishment of being exiled. One of the greatest battles ever recorded in the annals of time was that between the church and the empire. This battle lasted for 300 years with the church being triumphant. Jesus had assured His disciples that the gates of Hades would not prevail against His church (Matthew 16:18), but the picture was often bleak.

James Russell Lowell, a great American poet, in his poem "The Present Crisis" wrote,

> Truth forever on the scaffold
> Wrong forever on the throne,
> Yet that scaffold sways the future,
> And, behind the dim unknown,
> Standeth God within the shadow,
> Keeping watch above His own.

In William Cullen Bryant's poem, "The Battlefield," he gave assurance for the victory of truth:

> Truth though crushed to earth shall rise again.
> The eternal years of God are hers.
> But error wounded writhes in pain
> And dies among his worshipers.

The lines of the two poets accurately express the conflict between the empire and the church and the triumphant outcome of the church in the struggle.

In the fourth century of our era, Rome was ruled by the pagan emperor Julian, who ordered all the churches of the Nazarene (as he called them) be closed, and the closed pagan temples he reopened. En route to fight the Persians, he camped for some months near Antioch of Syria to further train his army and to provision it. While there, he heard that an old boyhood friend who had become a Christian was operating a store in Antioch. One day the emperor dressed as a civilian and went down to Antioch where he found his old friend. After visiting for a short time, he looked his friend in the eye and said, "As I came down to Antioch, I saw the pagan temples opened and hundreds of people entering them to worship, but the churches of the Nazarene were closed." Then looking his old friend in the eye, he asked sarcastically, "What is the carpenter of Nazareth doing these days?" The Christian looked the emperor in the eye and asked him, "Do you want to know?" The reply was a sarcastic, "Yes." The Christian replied, "He is building a coffin in which to bury your empire." In less than two years, the defeated emperor lay dying on his cot, just west of the Euphrates, and acknowledged, "Thou hast conquered, Galilean."

This is the message of the great book of Revelation: the assurance of the triumph of the kingdom of God. In the early part of the fourth century, Tertullian of North Africa truthfully observed, "The blood of the martyrs has become the seed of the church." Again, let us remind ourselves of the key verse of the book, Revelation 11:15: "The kingdoms of this world are become the kingdoms of our Lord, and of his Christ; and he shall reign for ever and ever." The book of Revelation is a book of victory. It teaches that the commander-in-chief of the greatest army ever marshaled on the fields of war will at last place the flag of victory on the everlasting hills of conquest when the church of God will have triumphed, when time will become eternity and earth, heaven.

CHAPTER I

"THE THINGS WHICH MUST SHORTLY COME TO PASS"

Revelation 1

The opening of Revelation reads, "The Revelation of Jesus Christ, which God gave unto him, to show unto his servants things which must shortly come to pass; and he sent and signified *it* by his angel unto his servant John." Revelation 22:6 states, "And he said unto me, These sayings *are* faithful and true: and the Lord God of the holy prophets sent his angel to show unto his servants the things which must shortly be done." The Greek word *engus*, here rendered "shortly come to pass," can also be rendered "must soon take place." These Scriptures, and others we could cite, indicate that the book of Revelation essentially addresses itself to current or approaching current conditions that concerned the Christians in the Roman world of his or her time. This opposes the approach of many would-be exegetes of the book who see it as concerned almost entirely with the future, even near to the end of the world, involving a rapture, an earthly reign of Christ, the battle of Armageddon ad infinitum.

As earlier stated, the immediate thrust of the message of the book of Revelation applied primarily to its day. Revelation 1:3, which reads, "for the time is at hand," further expresses this, as well as Revelation 22:10: "And he saith unto me, Seal not the sayings of the prophecy of this book: for the time is at hand." However, as will be seen in a further study of the time-table in Revelation, the message of the book addresses also future times, even to the end of time.

What kind of book is the book of Revelation? It is a *revelation*. The first word in it is *apokalupsis*, which is translated by the English word, "revelation." The best Greek-English dictionary, that by Arndt and Gingrich, who translated and adapted Bauer's monumental Greek New Testament Lexicon, defines it as (1) "the revelation of a truth," (2) "of revelation of a particular kind, through vision, etc.," (3) "the eschatological sense of the disclosure of secrets belonging to the last day." Briefly, the Greek word *apokalupsis* means revealing that which has been concealed or making known the unknown.

Some decades ago when I was the minister of the Central Church of Christ in Los Angeles, an interesting thing happened one Wednesday afternoon. The ladies of the church had met for Bible study, for lunch and to sew for the needy. I had walked out of my office for some fresh air when I found myself surrounded by a large number of police cars with policemen. While I was wondering the meaning of what I was seeing, a policeman approached me.

"Are you the minister of the church?" he asked. I replied in the affirmative. He stated, "The Bank of America on Pico, about two blocks away, has just been robbed, and the robber was last seen entering the side door of your church building. We are going to find him, and there will probably be a shoot out. We want you to go into your office and lock your doors securely." I replied, "There are a large number of women here for Bible study, for sewing and for lunch." He answered, "Get them into your office with you, and do not go out!"

We did not have to be persuaded! We stayed in there about 30 minutes and did not hear a shot. I ventured out and saw one remaining policeman, unsatisfied with the search and the failure to find the robber. He was standing beside the pulpit, and behind the pulpit were beautiful blue drawn curtains. The policeman pulled the cord on the curtains and before realizing it stepped into the baptistry, getting wet up to his shoulders.

The experience was an apocalypse, a revelation of what had been concealed from the policeman. That incident made the front page of two of the leading Los Angeles papers. As we study the apocalyptic parts of the book of Revelation through apocalyptic glasses, they will be easily understood and become very meaningful to the student, teacher and preacher. This approach will give meaning to many scriptures in Revelation and, at the same time, conceal meanings from those unprepared for the use of the apocalyptic approach.

The second major characteristic of the book of Revelation is that it is a *prophecy*. Revelation 1:3 states, "Blessed *is* he that readeth, and they that hear the words of this prophecy, and keep those things which are written therein: for the time *is* at hand." God told John in Revelation 10:11, "Thou must prophesy again before many peoples, and nations, and tongues, and kings." These words further establish that John was a prophet. Shortly before the pen of inspiration was laid aside, never to be taken up again, John wrote, "I testify unto every man that heareth the words of the prophecy of this book, If any man shall add unto these things, God shall add unto him the plagues that are written in this book: And if any man shall take away from the words of the book of this prophecy, God shall take away his part out of the book of life, and out of the holy city, and *from* the things which are written in this book" (Revelation 22:18-19).

Probably more than any other characteristic of Revelation, students have emphasized its prophetic character. What is prophecy? Multiplied millions of people do not understand the nature of prophecy, especially biblical prophecy. Many think it refers exclusively to the future, when, in reality, it deals with both the near-present and the future. The English word "prophecy" is a translation of a Greek word that means "a spokesman for another." In Revelation John is the spokesman for God. Prophecy also has the meaning of "to a day and of a day" as illustrated by the Old Testament prophets. John, the inspired writer of Revelation, wrote "of a day and to a day," of the present and the future. He went so far as to lift the telescope of prophecy and to look down the corridors of time and to write of future times and conditions. The Greek word translated "prophet" has its Hebrew counterpart in the word transliterated *navi*, which has as its basic meaning "one who cannot contain himself." His message is such that *he must speak*, as was the case of John.

During World War II, the governor of one of the states of the United States said that the prophet Isaiah predicted that there would be tire rationing during the war, citing Isaiah 3:18 to support his statement. The Scripture reads, "In that day the Lord will take away the bravery of *their* tinkling ornaments *about their feet*, and *their* cauls, and *their* round tires like the moon." The "round tires" were ornaments that looked like the moon. Worldly-minded women wore them. The governor took Isaiah's prediction out of its context and made a pretext of it to prove what he already believed. Isaiah the prophet spoke to the decadent Israelites of his time and not to the American people of World War II.

The third and probably most inclusive fact about the book of Revelation is that it is primarily a letter written to the seven churches of Asia Minor, named in Revelation 1:11, with the contents of the letters in Chapters 2 and 3. The text states, "John to the seven churches which are in Asia" (Revelation 1:4); and in 1:10-11, "I was in the Spirit on the Lord's day, and heard behind me a great voice, as of a trumpet, Saying, I am Alpha and Omega, the first and the last: and, What thou seest, write in a book, and send *it* unto the seven churches which are in Asia; unto Ephesus, and unto Smyrna, and unto Pergamos, and unto Thyatira, and unto Sardis, and unto Philadelphia, and unto Laodicea."

Across a number of centuries, there have been those who have believed that each of these seven churches represents a certain period in the history of the church. There is no supporting evidence for this belief in the text of the letters, in the book of Revelation as a whole or elsewhere, so far as the knowledge of your writer is concerned. The contents of the letters deal with conditions in each of the seven addressed churches. Furthermore, Chapters 1 and 4-22 speak to all Christians of that day and of all time.

Conservative scholarship generally acknowledges that the human author of the book of Revelation is John the apostle. The internal evidence of the book points to this fact. Five times in the book the author declares himself to be John. He does not call himself the apostle John, but he was so widely known that the original readers would have understood that he was John, the beloved disciple, the apostle of the Lord Jesus Christ.

Justin Martyr, in his *Dialogue with Trypho*, written in A.D. 155, affirmed that John wrote the book of Revelation. Irenaeus, a disciple of Polycarp, who was a disciple of the apostle John, wrote in the latter third of the second century that it was John who wrote the book of Revelation. Other external evidence, such as the writings of Clement of Alexandria and Origin of Alexandria, also testify that John was the human author of the book of Revelation.

The evidence for the date of the book of Revelation supports a date in the ninth decade of the first century. There are some students who claim the book was written in the sixth decade of the first century, but Irenaeus specifically says that John wrote the book of Revelation on the isle of Patmos during the reign of Domitian. Domitian reigned from A.D. 81 to A.D. 96 or 98. Not only do we have this external evidence for the date of Revelation, but the entire thrust of the book is against emperor worship, and emperor worship had not reached the point reflected in Revelation by the sixth decade. It had, however, reached that point by the ninth decade.

Let us begin a study of the text itself.

"The Revelation of Jesus Christ, which God gave unto him, to show unto his servants things which must shortly come to pass; and he sent and signified *it* by his angel unto his servant John" (1:1).

Here we have the lines of communication set out: first God, then the Lord Jesus Christ, then His angel, and then His servant the apostle John. It was not Jesus being revealed, but that which He would reveal. We must stress that the verse speaks of, "that which must shortly come to pass." If you read this in your newspaper, you would understand that it referred to something in the near future, not something that would happen in two thousand years. That these things "must shortly come to pass" is a key concept in understanding the book of Revelation.

"Who bare record of the word of God, and of the testimony of Jesus Christ, and of all things that he saw. Blessed *is* he that readeth, and they that hear the words of this prophecy, and keep those things which are written therein: for the time *is* at hand" (1:2-3).

The words "at hand" are a translation of the Greek word *engus*. This is the word used by our Lord, by John the Baptist, by the 70 whom Jesus sent out and by the Twelve. They said that the kingdom of heaven is "at hand," or just around the corner.

The Lord also promises a blessing to the one who reads these words. In Colossians 4:16, Paul requested that the Laodicean Christians read the letter addressed to the Colossians and that the Colossians read the letter from the Laodiceans. Adolph Harnack, a scholar of another generation, taught in the University of Berlin. In his book, *Bible Reading in the Early Church*, he showed conclusively that it was the practice of the churches of our Lord in the first and second centuries to assemble and hear the word of God read publicly to them. Today, a preacher often selects a text and preaches from it, but in New Testament times a reader read an entire book in the assembly and then made comment on the book.

"John to the seven churches which are in Asia: Grace *be* unto you, and peace, from him which is, and which was, and which is to come; and from the seven Spirits which are before his throne; And from Jesus Christ, *who is* the faithful witness, *and* the first begotten of the dead, and the prince of the kings of the earth" (1:4-5a).

John gives a common salutation as he addresses the seven churches. He offers "grace and peace." "Grace" is the translation of the Greek word *charis*, which means "favor or unmerited favor." It connotes happiness. Paul often used it as he addressed his epistles to the early Christians. The word "peace" translates the Greek word *eirene*, which is in turn a translation of the Hebrew word *shalom*, which Israelis still use as a word of greeting on the streets of Jerusalem. It is not only a greeting, but when fellow Jews tell each other good-bye, as they have since ancient times, they say "shalom" or "peace."

The Lord Jesus Christ "which is, and which was, and which is to come" offers this grace and peace. Revelation 1:8 says, **"I am Alpha and Omega, the beginning and the ending, saith the Lord, which is, and which was, and which is to come, the Almighty."** In 1:11, the Lord again refers to Himself as the Alpha and the Omega. "Alpha" is the first letter of the Greek alphabet, and "omega" is the last letter. By the use of these two words, the first and the last of the alphabet, the early Christians understood that the Lord Jesus Christ was the beginning and the ending and that He was continuous in existence. We read in John 1:1-2, "In the beginning was the Word, and the Word was with God, and the Word was God. The same was in the beginning with God." The tense of the original language here implies His continuous existence. In John 8:58, Jesus said, "Verily, verily, I say unto you, Before Abraham was, I am," implying His continuous existence, even before Abraham was born.

This was especially meaningful to the Christians in the seven churches. On every hand, they heard from their Roman neighbors, from the Romans they associated with in business and from the Romans they worked for day in and day out that "Rome is eternal."

The city of Rome is the "Eternal City." They heard, "All roads lead to Rome, and all roads lead out of Rome." Everything else was subject to time; everything else would go, but Rome would stay. Rome would stay forever and forever. But the Lord assured the Christians of Ephesus, Smyrna, Pergamum and the others of the seven churches that Jesus Christ was the Alpha and the Omega, the beginning and the end. Powerful men of the past, such as Sargon II, the Hitler of Assyria, were gone. The pharaohs of ancient Egypt were gone. Julius Caesar was gone. So many potentates have gone across the stage of history and are no more. But the Christians said, "The Lord Jesus Christ is forever. Let's follow Him; let's stay with Him. To whom can we go? It is only He that has the words of eternal life."

His greeting also was from the seven Spirits of God and from the Lord, who **"loved us, and washed us from our sins in his own blood, and hath made us kings and priests unto God and his Father; to him *be* glory and dominion for ever and ever. Amen"** (1:5b-6). Here is the first of many doxologies of praise to God and Jesus in Revelation. There are none to the Roman emperors.

"Behold, he cometh with clouds; and every eye shall see him, and they *also* which pierced him: and all kindreds of the earth shall wail because of him. Even so, Amen" (1:7).

So these Christians in the ninth decade of the Christian era heard the announcement of the second coming of our Lord. Men have repeated that announcement thousands of time through the centuries. Paul spoke of "looking for that blessed hope, and the glorious appearing of the great God and our Saviour Jesus Christ" (Titus 2:13), the hope of God's people down through the ages.

"I John, who also am your brother, and companion in tribulation, and in the kingdom and patience of Jesus Christ, was in the isle that is called Patmos, for the word of God, and for the testimony of Jesus Christ" (1:9).

John identifies himself to the Christians of Western Asia Minor as their brother. Not only is he their brother, but their companion or partaker in tribulation. John was no armchair editor. John had suffered with the Christians. He knew what it was to suffer as a Christian. He understood the words of Peter: "But let none of you suffer as a murderer, or *as* a thief, or *as* an evildoer, or as a busybody in other men's matters. Yet if *any man suffer* as a Christian, let him not be ashamed;

but let him glorify God on this behalf" (1 Peter 4:15-16).

Pliny later wrote a letter to the emperor Trajan, telling him that in his province of Bithynia, his authorities punished those who were followers of the Christ just because of who they were, rather than for anything they had done. John, "in the kingdom and patience of Jesus Christ, was in the isle that is called Patmos." The isle of Patmos is some 40 to 50 miles southwest of the great city of Ephesus, the fourth largest and most important city in the Roman Empire. Ephesus had been John's home, but Rome reserved the island of Patmos for a place to punish people. Rome banished its enemies, those considered seditious, to the island. They considered it seditious to refuse to worship the Roman emperor as Lord and God and thus the divinity of the empire. So they banished John to this isle because he refused to worship Domitian and probably his predecessors, Titus and Vespasian, and others.

John, external evidence tells us, worked in the mines of Patmos. This island is only six miles wide and 10 miles wide. It was a volcanic island and a Roman penitentiary. John was a very old man while he was there, probably in his 90s. His back, without doubt, was bent. His face was furrowed with the marks of time. His eyes must have been dim, and his walk must have been faltering; but still the Romans made him work. John was there "for the word of God, and for the testimony of Jesus Christ." He had testified that Jesus Christ is Lord and God and had borne witness to the saviorhood of Christ in his own life and in the lives of multiplied hundreds of thousands of others.

"I was in the Spirit on the Lord's day" (1:10a).

The Lord's day was a day that was special and belonged to the Lord. The Lord requires the first of everything, and He requires the first day of the week in the Christian dispensation. In early Christian literature on this side of the first century, we have a number of great Christian leaders who testify that the early Christians met on the Lord's day, the first day of the week, to worship God in spirit and in truth. Now what does it mean that John was "in the Spirit on the Lord's day"? It signifies that he was oblivious to things that were around him. He was in communion with the Lord Jesus Christ. He was the receptacle that was receiving the great message of the book of Revelation.

He writes, **"I heard behind me a great voice, as of a trumpet, Saying, I am Alpha and Omega, the first and the last: and, What thou seest, write in a book, and send** *it* **unto the seven churches which are in Asia; unto Ephesus, and unto Smyrna, and unto Pergamos, and unto Thyatira, and unto Sardis, and unto Philadelphia, and unto Laodicea"** (1:10b-11).

John addresses his message to these seven specific churches. Since John spoke to seven churches, we know that this number of perfection (seven) means that he is also addressing the whole church, the complete church. His audience is specifically the seven churches of Western Asia Minor, and also the whole church. He is speaking to the church of Jerusalem, of Antioch, of Alexandria and of Rome. But he has to draw the line somewhere, so he names the seven churches that are his primary audience.

"And I turned to see the voice that spake with me. And being turned, I saw seven golden candlesticks" (1:12).

These seven golden candlesticks or lampstands are representative of the traditional Jewish seven-branched lampstands called the menorah. In verse 20 the Lord identifies these candlesticks as the seven churches, churches that were to be a light to their world.

Next John sees a vision of the Son of man, drawn from the Old Testament. **"And in the midst of the seven candlesticks** *one* **like unto the Son of man, clothed with a garment down to the foot, and girt about the paps with a golden girdle. His head and** *his* **hairs** *were* **white like wool, as white as snow; and his eyes** *were* **as a flame of fire; And his feet like unto fine brass, as if they burned in a furnace; and his voice as the sound of many waters. And he had in his right hand seven stars: and out of his mouth went a sharp two-edged sword: and his countenance** *was* **as the sun shineth in his strength"** (1:13-16).

The "Son of man" was Jesus' favorite self-designation. "I saw in the night visions, and, behold, *one* like the Son of man came with the clouds of heaven, and came to the Ancient of days, and they brought him near before him" (Daniel 7:13).

The clothing the Son of man wears comes from the vestments of the high priest as described in the book of Exodus. His white hair indicates his eternity and the wisdom that comes with maturity. His eyes as flaming fire and feet like fine brass are symbols of his knowledge and wisdom and strength. His voice as the sound of many waters is a voice of power and authority, as the sound of the rumbling of water such as Niagara Falls. Verse 20 identifies the stars in his right hand as the angels of the seven churches. His words were powerful and discerning, as the word of God. "For the word of God *is* quick, and powerful, and sharper than any two-edged sword, piercing even to the dividing asunder of soul and spirit, and of the joints and marrow, and *is* a discerner of the thoughts and intents of the heart" (Hebrews 4:12). His face shone like the sun, like Moses when he came down from Sinai. "And it came to pass, when Moses came down from mount Sinai with the two tables of testimony in Moses' hand, when he came down from the mount, that Moses wist not that the skin of his face shone while he talked with him. And when Aaron and all the children of Israel saw Moses, behold, the skin of his face shone; and they were afraid to come nigh him" (Exodus 34:29-30).

"And when I saw him, I fell at his feet as dead. And he laid his right hand upon me, saying unto me, Fear not; I am the first and the last: I *am* he that liveth, and was dead; and, behold, I am alive for evermore, Amen; and have the keys of hell and of death" (1:17-18).

John's reaction was tremendous fear at the overwhelming vision before him, but the Lord, who has conquered death, has come to calm fears and offer hope. The message is a message of faith and hope and victory, not one of fear.

John received a commission to **"write the things which thou hast seen, and the things which are, and the things which shall be hereafter"** (1:19).

Thinking of what he has seen, we go back with John to July 19, in the year A.D. 64, as the city of Rome experienced its greatest fire, one of the greatest fires of all time. This fire swept the whole city, as tenement houses by the score burned to ashes. The fire forced the occupants of the houses out into the streets seeking safety. Children ran in horror into the streets seeking their parents, unable to find them. The imperial palace itself was subject to this great conflagration. The dead who burned could not be numbered. After the city burned, the question was, "Who started the fire? Who is to blame?" By this time the emperor Nero had come into disfavor by the Roman people, so they began to wonder if he had caused the fire. They knew that he dreamed of building Rome anew as beautiful as ancient Athens. So Nero was uneasy, wondering what he would do to deflect the blame.

In the midst of Nero's conflict, his Jewish wife Poppaea whispered in his ear, "Why don't you say the Christians set the city of Rome on fire. Have they not been preaching that this old world is going to burn up, and that there will be a new city. Just accuse them of setting the city on fire and the people will believe it." Nero spread the accusation, quickly convincing the people that the Christians had set the fires. Nero took advantage of the situation and persecuted the Christians without mercy. He would have the women, virtually nude, thrown on the horns of ferocious bulls and torn to pieces in the sight of the merciless people. He would dress Christians in the skins of animals and have them torn apart by wild, ferocious hounds. He would have the Christians thrown to the lions. Over time, his slogan, "The Christians to the lions!" became increasingly popular. So Christians without number were thrown to the lions and burned at the stake.

The spectacle came to a great climax when Nero staged a tremendous night show in his gardens. He invited all Rome to see the Christians burn. His men placed stakes along Nero's race course. They wrapped rags saturated with oil around Christians, and then placed them on the stakes. At a certain time, Nero, with his charioteer driving his chariot, drove through his race course. He set the Christians on fire one by one, so that they all ignited in a tunic of pain. As their ashes fell to the ground, their spirits took their flight unto God who gave them. As one spectacle after another befell the Christians, it finally became too much even for the Roman stomach. As Renan has said, "For the first time in human history there was sensitivity to real moral purity." The last words the Christians heard were the words of reviling from the people of Rome.

I shall never forget the experience of walking around the race course of Nero in March of 1974. Cold chills ran up and down my spine as I visualized the Christians who gave their lives so that you and I and multiplied millions of children of God might have the seed of the kingdom in the church of the living God.

Not only did John think of the horrors caused by the burning of Rome, but he must have thought of the death of the apostle Peter.

Eusebius, the first reliable church historian, and the *Acts of Peter*, another ancient book, tell that as Peter preached at Rome he converted some of the concubines of some of the highest powers in Rome. These concubines decided to live lives of purity, for which their masters severely persecuted them. They persecuted Peter himself, and they sought his life. Friends warned him to escape from Rome. But as the story goes, as he was leaving Rome he met the Lord. He said to the Lord, "Where goest thou Lord?" "Quo vadis?" The Lord said, "I'm going into Rome to die." Peter said, "Are you going to die again?" The Lord replied, "Yes, I am going to be crucified again." Upon that, the story goes, Peter turned around and went back to Rome himself. They crucified his wife without mercy in his very presence. As she was dying, he said to her, "Remember our Lord." When the time came for his crucifixion, Peter requested that he be crucified, not head upwards, but head downward. He said that he was not worthy to be crucified the same way his Lord had been crucified.

Without doubt as John thought of what he had seen, he thought of the death of Paul. Again I remember a hot August day in the summer of 1948 and a visit to the Mamertine Prison in ancient Rome. We made our way down the winding stairway to the bottom, which was very damp and cold. We remembered how Paul wrote to Timothy urging him to bring his cloak he had left in Troas, the cloak wet with the brine of the Aegean and the Mediterranean, the cloak yellow with the dust of the Egnatian Way, the cloak white with the snows of Pamphylia and Phrygia, and the cloak red with the blood of the apostle Paul.

The time came for Paul to stand before Nero who condemned him to die. From his prison cell, he looked out through his little window across the Aegean and the Mediterranean to ancient Ephesus where he had left the young preacher Timothy. He wrote, "I am now ready to be offered, and the time of my departure is at hand. I have fought a good fight, I have finished my course, I have kept the faith: Henceforth there is laid up for me a crown of righteousness, which the Lord, the righteous judge, shall give me at that day: and not to me only, but unto all them also that love his appearing" (2 Timothy 4:6-8). They led Paul out of his prison cell, through the beautiful marble columns holding up the imperial palace and down the Appian

Way. Friends like Luke and Linus and Timothy followed close by. As they traveled on, the Romans stopped to scourge Paul again and again. Then Paul placed his head on the Roman anvil. The ax of the Roman soldier glistened in the sun as he lifted it high and brought it down with full force to sever the head of the apostle Paul. In his death, Paul was more alive than he had ever been before.

These were things John must have had in mind as he wrote the things he had seen. He was also to write "the things which are," referring to the things in Revelation 1-5. The "things which shall be hereafter" refer to the events of chapters 6-22.

The last verse of the chapter explains the seven golden candlesticks and the seven stars.

"The mystery of the seven stars which thou sawest in my right hand, and the seven golden candlesticks. The seven stars are the angels of the seven churches: and the seven candlesticks which thou sawest are the seven churches" (1:20).

The angels of the seven churches are more than likely the ministers of the individual congregations. The word angel means messenger, and the ministers would naturally share the messages of the Lord with their congregations.

CHAPTER 2

LETTERS TO EPHESUS, SMYRNA, PERGAMOS AND THYATIRA

Revelation 2

Ephesus was the fourth most important city in the Roman Empire. Rome was first, followed by Alexandria and Antioch of Syria. Ephesus sat at the mouth of the Cayster River that flowed into the Aegean Sea. Trade from the Far East, the Far West, the Far South and the Far North met in Ephesus making it a great commercial city. It was also a great governmental city since the provincial governor resided there. Ephesus was also a great educational center and a religious center. Acts 19 tells of Paul's experiences in Ephesus.

Paul found 12 men who had been baptized with the baptism of John. They had not received the Holy Spirit or even heard that God had given the Holy Spirit. They were baptized in the name of Christ and received the Holy Spirit. Then Paul began to teach in the synagogue of Ephesus. For three months he reasoned from the Old Testament every Sabbath day that Jesus was the Messiah. After three months, the Jews drove him out of the synagogue, and he then entered greater opportunity.

Paul went into the city and continued to dispute in the school of Tyrannus. According to the Codex Beza, one of the best manuscripts of the book of Acts, he taught the word of the Lord from 10 in the morning until 4 in the afternoon. The result of Paul's teaching was that all Asia heard the word of the Lord and believed. Thus, through his teaching at the school of Tyrannus, he established the churches in Colossae, Smyrna, Thyatira, Pergamum, Philadelphia, Sardis, Laodicea and Magnesia, Hierapolis and throughout western Asia

Minor. Paul's teaching continued for 18 months. Then Paul engaged in exorcism. He met some Jewish exorcists, but Paul's casting out demons far surpassed what they could do. Thus the people understood that Paul was the man of God and not the exorcists. As a result, they burned their magical books worth 50,000 pieces of silver. "So mightily grew the word of God and prevailed" (Acts 19:20).

Paul continued preaching that God is not a God worshiped with things made with the hands of men, but He is an invisible God in whom we live and move and have our being. Because of Paul's preaching, the business of Demetrius and his fellow silversmiths, who were making images of Diana, decreased markedly. Their income fell so sharply that they started a great riot in Ephesus. They went up and down the streets of the city, shouting, "Great is Diana of the Ephesians! Great is Diana of the Ephesians!" The whole city got into an uproar. The town clerk called the free citizens of the city together into the *ecclesia*, or common assembly of the free citizens. He reprimanded them for the riot they had caused. He said to them, "Do we not know that Diana of the Ephesians is great, and that all Asia worships Diana of the Ephesians? Why are you causing this riot and commotion? If this gets up to the higher powers, it will be bad for all of us." Paul wanted to go into the theatre (seating 25,000), but his close friends would not let him. "You'd better not go, for if you do, you'll likely be slaughtered in the theatre." The mob probably would have killed him if he had gone in. From this beginning he established the church in Ephesus.

In Acts 20, Paul called together the elders of the church at Ephesus to meet him at Miletus. He could not go to Ephesus because the Cayster River had risen and overflowed its banks. Among other things, he told them, "I have not shunned to declare unto you all the counsel of God. Take heed therefore unto yourselves, and to all the flock, over the which the Holy Ghost hath made you overseers, to feed the church of God, which he hath purchased with his own blood. For I know this, that after my departing shall grievous wolves enter in among you, not sparing the flock" (Acts 20:27-29).

The book of Ephesians has six chapters that set forth the magnificence and grandeur of the church of the living God. Besides the biblical letter to the Ephesians, we also have the letter of Ignatius of Antioch to the church of God in Ephesus written about A.D. 117

as he was one his way to Rome to meet his death by lions. These two letters shed more light on the situation of the church at Ephesus as addressed in Revelation.

The Lord's Revelation letter begins, **"Unto the angel of the church of Ephesus write"** (2:1a). We do not know the identity of this "angel," but it likely was Timothy, whom Paul left in Ephesus to set things in order.

"These things saith he that holdeth the seven stars in his right hand, who walketh in the midst of the seven golden candlesticks" (2:1b). He who held the seven stars in His right hand was none other than the Lord Jesus Christ. The last verse of the first chapter tells us the seven stars are the angels of the seven churches. The Lord has promised, "Lo, I am with you alway, *even* unto the end of the world. Amen" (Matthew 28:20). So our Lord held in the hollow of His hand the angel of the church in Ephesus. The candlesticks that the Lord walked among were the churches who held the candle, who held the light. Our Lord said, "Ye are the light of the world" (Matthew 5:14). Paul told the Philippians, "Do all things without murmurings and disputings: That ye may be blameless and harmless, the sons of God, without rebuke, in the midst of a crooked and perverse nation, among whom ye shine as lights in the world" (Philippians 2:14-15).

The Lord writes to the Ephesian Christians, **"I know thy works, and thy labour, and thy patience, and how thou canst not bear them which are evil: and thou hast tried them which say they are apostles, and are not, and hast found them liars. And hast borne, and hast patience, and for my name's sake hast laboured, and hast not fainted"** (2:2-3).

The word "know" here is the Greek word *oida*. There is another Greek word, *ginosko*, which conveys a knowledge possessed upon gaining certain information, but *oida* conveys a knowledge that is divine, that is superhuman. The Lord knew the works of the Ephesian Christians. All things were naked and laid open before the eyes of him with whom we have to do. He knew their works, and he also knew their labor, their toil, their hard work. He knew their patience. In 2 Peter 1 patience is one of the rungs of the ladder that stretches from earth to heaven. Repeatedly the New Testament urges the children of God to possess patience.

Those Ephesians Christians had also tried itinerant preachers who had claimed to be gospel preachers. They went up and down the Roman world claiming to have the gladsome news of the gospel, but in reality they did not have it. Their gospel was a perverted gospel, which was not really a gospel. It was another gospel. They claimed to be sound in the faith, to be loyal to the truth, but the elders of the Ephesian church examined them and found them to be false apostles, false preachers and false messengers.

The Lord highly commended this church in Ephesus. Few congregations of the Lord's church would have higher commendation than the church in Ephesus. But there was something terribly wrong in Ephesus. The Lord said, **"Nevertheless I have *somewhat* against thee, because thou hast left thy first love"** (2:4).

Jeremiah pleaded for the children of God to return to Jehovah. He told them they had foresaked the God they had married on Mt. Sinai. God had been faithful across the centuries, but He asks, "Can a maid forget her ornaments or a bride her attire? Yet my people have forgotten me days without number" (Jeremiah 2:32 KJV).

Leaving one's first love is a tragic thing. It is often a gradual thing. You have seen couples beautifully and happily married starting out in life together hand in hand, arm in arm, heart in heart, devoted to each other, loving one another. But as the years and the decades pass, their interests become different and they grow apart. Longer and longer as time goes on, they grow farther and farther apart, until down the way, sometimes even toward the sunset of life, they have lost their first love. That is the tragedy of tragedies, but a tragedy that is even greater is to see a member of the Lord's church who has lost his first love for his Lord. When he became a Christian he would not think of missing a worship service. He contributed cheerfully and generously. He prayed regularly. He was faithful in all the work of the church. But as the years passed, the world came into his life and gradually increased and began to dwell more and more in him until he had forsaken the church. He left his first love and went the way of the world. Sometimes a church will do the same thing. The church in Sardis did that.

Some churches are like that. I have visited some churches with a reputation for being sound, and I have found them sound — sound asleep. They have left their first love. "Ichabod" ("the glory is departed," 1 Samuel 4:21) could almost be written over their door. The church at Ephesus had left its first love. The members no longer sang as they used to sing. They no longer contributed as they did in the early years of their Christian life. They didn't read the Bible as they used to. They didn't pray as they did when they were first Christians. That truly is the tragedy of tragedies.

Our Lord wrote to them, **"Remember therefore from whence thou art fallen, and repent, and do the first works; or else I will come unto thee quickly, and will remove thy candlestick out of his place, except thou repent"** (2:5).

Memory is a great thing. If it were not for memory, the prodigal son would not have returned to the home of his father. If it had not been for memory, the memory of a mother, the memory of a wife, the memory of children, how many men would have gone the way of all the earth? How many women have gone the same way? O, how blessed it is to think about what memory can do. So the Lord told the Ephesians, "Remember therefore from whence thou art fallen, and repent, and do the first works." Start where you left, where you began to fall away, where you began to leave; start all over again in the land of beginning again.

"But this thou hast, that thou hatest the deeds of the Nicolaitanes, which I also hate" (2:6).

Now who were these Nicolaitanes? They were the followers of Nicolaus, a proselyte of ancient Antioch, who was a devotee of Balaam and Balak. The chief tenets of their doctrine were fornication and eating things sacrificed to idols. Fornication was quite prevalent in the world of the first century. Every sailor, and there were multiplied thousands of them because the Roman Empire relied upon sea trade, had his girl in every port. Eating meat sacrificed to idols was also a very common practice. There were Nicolaitanes in Ephesus, but the Christians hated their deeds. They would not have anything to do with them.

"He that hath an ear, let him hear what the Spirit saith unto the churches; To him that overcometh will I give to eat of the tree of life, which is in the midst of the paradise of God" (2:7).

The admonition, "He that hath an ear, let him hear what the Spirit saith unto the churches," rings clear as a bell in every letter to the seven churches. Every letter also gives a promise to the overcomer.

That was a tremendous promise for those early Christians because life was hard. Temptations were great. Many tried to force them to worship the Roman emperor, but they were strong enough to overcome and not worship him.

The Lord promised the Ephesian Christians they could eat of the tree of life. God took away the tree of life in the Garden of Eden from Adam and Eve and all mankind. The cherubim guarded the entrance to the garden, so that no one could eat of the tree of life. In eternity a beautiful river of water of life will flow from the throne of God, sending forth its silvery sprays at the feet of the redeemed. On either side of this river the tree of life will grow. It will yield its fruit every month, and it will be for the healing of the nations. They that overcome will have the glorious privilege of eating of the tree of life, which is in the very midst of the paradise of God. It is no marvel that Paul wrote to the Ephesians, "Blessed *be* the God and Father of our Lord Jesus Christ, who hath blessed us with all spiritual blessings in heavenly *places* in Christ" (Ephesians 1:3). What a great church the church in Ephesus was, a church that must have reclaimed its first love, a church that must have become more dedicated and more devoted than ever to the cause of Christ.

This is the great church that lasted for a long time. It was a great religious center. It was the third great missionary center of the Roman Empire, from which Christians took the gospel to every nook and corner of the Roman world.

Smyrna was located 40 miles north of Ephesus, on the eastern end of a 30-mile long harbor, one of the most beautiful and productive harbors of its time. It was also on the end of a trade route that ran to the north and to the east from Smyrna across central Asia Minor to other commercial areas. The land around Smyrna was exceedingly fertile. The city itself was important in first century Roman history. It always allied itself with Rome in any conflicts with neighboring nations. In A.D. 23 Smyrna vied with Ephesus and Pergamum for the privilege of erecting a temple to Tiberius Caesar. Smyrna won the contest and erected an imperial temple dedicated to Tiberius Caesar, the contemporary emperor, and to his mother, Julia.

Smyrna was a very religious city, filled with religious people as Ephesus was. What Diana was to the Ephesians, Dionysius was to the Smyrnans. Dionysius, also known as Bacchus, was the god of wine. Much immorality came out of this religion. Much of the immorality of Smyrna and the surrounding area came as a result of the worship of Dionysius. The imperial cult was also prominent in Smyrna. Many Jews in Smyrna were important in city affairs. The city had at least one synagogue.

Smyrna was a beautiful city with a golden street that ran from one end of the city to the other. It had wide streets that met each other at right angles. On Mount Pagos, it had a theatre that seated 20,000 people, a very large theatre for that time. Smyrna was a very large and important city. The Muslim city of Izmir, Turkey, now stands where ancient Smyrna stood.

"And unto the angel of the church in Smyrna write" (2:8a).

The angel is again unknown to us but in all probability was Polycarp, a disciple of the apostle John. Polycarp became the 12th of 12 martyrs for the cause of Christ from Smyrna.

Polycarp was a highly revered Christian living in Smyrna and serving as one of the bishops of the congregation. He was an example of faithfulness to all who knew him. About A.D. 167, the Roman powers decided they were going to force Polycarp to renounce Christ and worship the Roman emperor or be put to death.

When Polycarp learned of this, close friends advised him to leave the city. He went out into the country about four miles to the home of one of the church members. Herod, the chief of police, heard of his whereabouts and went to find him. He knocked at the door of the place where Polycarp was staying and said, "I am here for Polycarp. I am going to arrest him and take him back to Smyrna." Polycarp came out, and Herod arrested him. The chief of police then forced him into the chariot and started to Smyrna.

Along the way, the chief told Polycarp, "When we get to the theatre in Smyrna, if you will deny Jesus Christ to be Lord and God and will confess the Roman emperor as Lord and God, you will live. If you refuse, you will die." When they arrived at the theatre in Smyrna, the riotous mob of Greeks, Romans, Egyptians and Jews cried, "The Christians to the lions! The Christians to the lions!"

Polycarp lifted his right hand and a profound silence settled over the crowd. In a firm voice Polycarp said, "Eighty and six years have I served Him, and I will not deny him now!" The bloodthirsty mob shouted, "Polycarp to the lions! Polycarp to the lions!" The sun had already set over the hills of Asia Minor, however, and it was the law of Rome that the lions' den closed at sunset. What would they do with Polycarp? There was only one thing left to do, burn him at the stake. Although it was now the Sabbath, the Jews eagerly gathered the wood for the fire. They placed Polycarp at the stake and began to tie him. He said, "Don't tie me. He who has stood by me through all of these years will stand by me now." As the sparks went upward, the spirit of Polycarp took its flight to God, and his ashes went down to the earth from which he had come. In his martyrdom, Polycarp was more alive that day than he had ever been. The story of the faith of Polycarp spread throughout the Roman world. It is no marvel that Tertullian in the second century wrote that "the blood of the martyrs is the seed of the church."

"These things saith the first and the last, which was dead, and is alive" (2:8b).

Let us imagine we are in the congregation in Smyrna. The reader of the congregation stands and reads this letter to the church. As we heard these words we would think of our neighbors, business associates and fellow laborers who asserted that Rome is eternal. But here the Lord of heavens wrote that it is not Rome, not the Roman emperors nor the Roman Senate, but it is the Lord Jesus Christ who is the Alpha and the Omega, the beginning and the end. When all the empires of the world have ceased, when the nations of the earth shall be sleeping in the solemn silence of the eternal dust, the church of the living God, the empire of God, will march continually and triumphantly on.

Not only was He who wrote to them the first and the last, but He was the One who was dead but lived again. He was incarcerated in a borrowed tomb, the tomb of Joseph of Arimathea. The Roman hierarchy saw that Romans guarded the tomb minute by minute and hour by hour for three days and three nights lest the disciples of Jesus steal Him away and report him being raised from the dead. In spite of the Roman seal placed upon the tomb and the Roman guards who watched over the tomb without a broken minute, Jesus broke the bars of death and came out triumphant over the tomb, bringing life and immortality and light to the gospel. So to the Smyrna Christians this was an encouraging message.

"I know thy works, and tribulation, and poverty, (but thou art rich)" (2:9a).
The Lord knew their works, as He knew the works of the Ephesians. He also knew their tribulations. The Greek word translated "tribulation" comes from a word describing the tramping of sugar cane to make molasses. The tramping of the feet was the "tribulation" of the cane. The persecution the Christians of Smyrna faced was intense. The Lord also knew their poverty and riches. The riches He referred to were the riches of the church of the living God. James wrote, "Hearken, my beloved brethren, Hath not God chosen the poor of this world rich in faith, and heirs of the kingdom which he hath promised to them that love him?" (James 2:5). The New Testament emphasizes this idea throughout. We have known many who have been poor in the world's goods but rich in faith. All of God's spiritual blessings are for his children, for we are the children of God, and God owns the universe.

"I know **the blasphemy of them which say they are Jews, and are not, but** *are* **the synagogue of Satan"** (2:9b).
Here is an indeed regrettable fact highlighted; among the greatest opponents of the church across the first three hundred years of its existence were the Jews. Many books have documented this fact. It surfaces in other places in the New Testament. These Jews claimed to be a true synagogue of Almighty God, but they were a synagogue of Satan. The Jews served as allies for the Romans in persecuting the Christians.

Our Lord had the comforting words, **"Fear none of those things which thou shalt suffer: behold, the devil shall cast *some* of you into prison, that ye may be tried; and ye shall have tribulation ten days: be thou faithful unto death, and I will give thee a crown of life"** (2:10).
These 10 days of tribulation were to be a short period of time, not a literal 10 days. There were some Christians under such extreme pressure that they faced death. Some denied their faith in Jesus Christ and confessed the Roman emperor as Lord and God. They apostatized, became unfaithful. Our Lord urged the Christians of Smyrna to be faithful unto death. Throughout God's Word, particularly the New Testament, faithfulness is encouraged and commanded for acceptance in the sight of God.

During a debate between a denominational preacher and a gospel preacher, the former said, "The time is coming when the leading men in the churches of Christ will depart from the doctrine of baptism for the remission of sins." Our brother readily responded, "I agree. The time likely will come when leading men will do that. But the time will never come when *faithful* men will depart from baptism for the remission of sins."

When I was a boy, I had to commit a poem to memory:

> The boy stood on the burning deck,
> Whence all but him had fled.
> The flames around the battle wreck
> Shone 'round them for the dead.

The thrust of the poem was and is that this boy was faithful to the end, faithful to the assignment given to him. You may have been to Yellowstone National Park to see "Old Faithful." In a split second he will erupt. He will not disappoint you. He is there on the split second because he is "Old Faithful." Faithfulness is commended not only in the Bible but in the affairs of men.

The Lord promised the crown of life to the faithful in Smyrna. The Smyrnans were very familiar with the runners in the Olympic games, who received a crown of victory. The Olympic crown was a fading one, though, and the crown received for being faithful to Christ unto death is the crown of life. It will last beyond time, beyond earthly life throughout eternity.

"He that hath an ear, let him hear what the Spirit saith unto the churches; He that overcometh shall not be hurt of the second death" (2:11). Revelation 20:15 tells us that the second death is the lake of fire. The lake of fire, of course, is hell itself. He who overcomes will escape hell. In each of the seven letters, commendation and reward are always given to the overcomer.

Pergamos or Pergamum, like Smyrna, was a very important city. Its library was then the second largest in the world, second only to Alexandria in Egypt. At Pergamum craftsmen developed vellum for books. Papyrus, produced in Egypt, had been the primary material used for books, but with the development of vellum, or parchment, it became more widely used because it was more permanent and not as fragile as papyrus.

Pergamum is the city with Satan's throne. **"And to the angel of the church in Pergamos write; These things saith he which hath the sharp sword with two edges"** (2:12).

The sharp sword with two edges sends us to Hebrews 4:12 to read, "The word of God *is* quick, and powerful, and sharper than any two-edged sword, piercing even to the dividing asunder of soul and spirit, and of the joints and marrow, and *is* a discerner of the thoughts and intents of the heart." In Ephesians 6:17, as the Christian is clad as one of the Christian army of God, he is to take the sword of the spirit, which is the word of God and the shield of faith to quench the fiery darts of the evil one. Rome was a military empire, known for her infantry's short sword. But no Roman sword could compare to the sword of the Lord.

"I know thy works and where thou dwellest, *even* where Satan's seat *is*" (2:13a). The Lord speaks of Satan's seat or throne because there was a very large imperial cult in Pergamum. The worship of the Roman emperor was rampant as well as the worship of other pagan gods. The people of Pergamum had built a huge altar to Zeus, the chief god of the Greeks and Romans. I shall never forget the visit to Pergamum and the oblong-shaped altar built to Zeus and the temple built to the Roman emperor.

Pergamum was a very religious city. It was Satan who was behind all of these expressions of religion, though. The Lord recognized that Satan had his throne right in Pergamum. He said, "I know where you dwell and that it is not easy there." Our Lord was mindful of the reality that it was very difficult to be a Christian in the city of Pergamum.

"Thou holdest fast my name, and hast not denied my faith, even in those days wherein Antipas *was* my faithful martyr, who was slain among you, where Satan dwelleth" (2:13b). This is all we know about Antipas, but it is enough. He has lived in the annals of time as a faithful witness, a martyr to the Lord Jesus Christ.

"But I have a few things against thee, because thou hast there them that hold the doctrine of Balaam, who taught Balak to cast a stumblingblock before the children of Israel, to eat things sacrificed unto idols, and to commit fornication. So hast thou also them that hold the doctrine of the Nicolaitanes, which thing I hate" (2:14-15).

The two most prominent sins in the Greco-Roman world of the first century were eating meats sacrificed to idols and committing fornication. Paul had to deal with the problem a number of times, especially in lascivious and lustful Corinth. There were those in the church in Pergamum who were looking upon these sins with toleration. The doctrine of the Nicolaitanes was closely akin to the teachings of Balaam and Balak.

"Repent; or else I will come unto thee quickly, and will fight against them with the sword of my mouth" (2:16).

The Lord warned, "I tell you, Nay: but, except ye repent, ye shall all likewise perish." (Luke 13:3, 5). So it was for the Pergamum Christians as it had been for the Ephesian Christians.

"He that hath an ear, let him hear what the Spirit saith unto the churches; To him that overcometh will I give to eat of the hidden manna, and will give him a white stone, and in the stone a new name written, which no man knoweth saving he that receiveth it" (2:17).

The hidden manna points to the manna given to the children of Israel during their forty years of wilderness wandering under the leadership of Moses. Being given a white stone was meaningful for all the members of the church because they knew that the victor received it as a prize. The contest here was that great race in which all of God's children have been engaged in down through the centuries. The overcomer receives the new name in the stone.

We don't know as much about the city of Thyatira as we do the other six cities. When I was at the site, it was a thriving Turkish town. All of these seven cities are in Turkey. We did not see any archaeological remains of first century Thyatira. We read in Acts 16 of Lydia, a seller of purple from Thyatira. She was a businesswoman and a religious woman because she sought a place to worship in Philippi, even though she was very far from home. As a stranger in Philippi, she could have hidden her identity, but she chose rather to make herself known and to seek out the worship to God. The purple dye of Thyatira was very much sought after and was very expensive, available only to those who were highly affluent.

"And unto the angel of the church in Thyatira write; These things saith the Son of God, who hath his eyes like unto a flame of fire, and his feet are like fine brass" (2:18).

Eyes like a flame of fire indicate His omniscience. He knows everything and is also omnipresent or everywhere. It was David who said, "Whither shall I go from thy spirit? or whither shall I flee from thy presence? If I ascend up into heaven, thou *art* there: if I make my bed in hell, behold, thou *art there*. If I take the wings of the morning, *and* dwell in the uttermost parts of the sea; Even there shall thy hand lead me, and thy right hand shall hold me" (Psalm 139:7-10). So the Lord reminded the Thyatira Christians, I am He who has eyes like a flame of fire, and my feet are solid. There is a solidarity to them that is not like Rome, which is here today but will be gone tomorrow.

"I know thy works, and charity, and service, and faith, and thy patience, and thy works; and the last *to be* more than the first" (2:19).

This is just the opposite of the conditions in Ephesus.

"Notwithstanding I have a few things against thee, because thou sufferest that woman Jezebel, which calleth herself a prophetess, to teach and to seduce my servants to commit fornication, and to eat things sacrificed unto idols" (2:20).

This Jezebel is like the Jezebel who was the wife of Ahab. A Tyrian princess, she brought the Tyrian worship of Baal into Israel and had Elijah as her great opponent. She and Elijah clashed repeatedly. It was not the literal Jezebel but her children who were working in the church in Thyatira. They were doctrinally and spiritually her children. They were teaching the servants of God to commit fornication and eat things sacrificed to idols.

"And I gave her space to repent of her fornication; and she repented not. Behold, I will cast her into a bed, and them that commit adultery with her into great tribulation, except they repent of their deeds. And I will kill her children with death; and all the churches shall know that I am he which searcheth the reins and hearts: and I will give unto every one of you according to your works" (2:21-23).

The Lord had this stern warning to Jezebel and her followers because of the tremendous damage they were doing in the church. The Lord would not allow the Thyatirans to compromise with her or allow her to continue, so destructive were her doctrines. The Lord's patience had run out.

47

"But unto you I say, and unto the rest in Thyatira, as many as have not this doctrine, and which have not known the depths of Satan, as they speak; I will put upon you none other burden. But that which ye have *already* hold fast till I come. And he that overcometh, and keepeth my works unto the end, to him will I give power over the nations: And he shall rule them with a rod of iron; as the vessels of a potter shall they be broken to shivers: even as I received of my Father. And I will give him the morning star. He that hath an ear, let him hear what the Spirit saith unto the churches" (2:24-29).

The Lord was conscious of not overburdening the Christians of Thyatira, but He wanted them to hold fast. This church whose last works were more than her first needed to stand firm. The Lord promised the overcomer power with Him, as He rules with His rod of iron. The second psalm, a Messianic psalm, warns that the kings of the earth will not stand against the Messiah. "I will declare the decree: the LORD hath said unto me, Thou *art* my Son; this day have I begotten thee. Ask of me, and I shall give *thee* the heathen *for* thine inheritance, and the uttermost parts of the earth *for* thy possession. Thou shalt break them with a rod of iron; thou shalt dash them in pieces like a potter's vessel" (Psalm 2:7-9). The morning star heralds the coming of the day and represents Christ, who is the brightest of all the stars. "I Jesus have sent mine angel to testify unto you these things in the churches. I am the root and the offspring of David, *and* the bright and morning star" (Revelation 22:16).

CHAPTER 3

LETTERS TO SARDIS, PHILADELPHIA AND LAODICEA

Revelation 3

As with Ephesus and Smyrna, Sardis, the fifth of the seven cities was a very great city. It was a great governmental center before Rome took over. It was a very wealthy city. And one of its kings, Croesus, was so wealthy that he was the model for the legend of King Midas who had the golden touch. He was literally a multi-millionaire. The river Pactolus, which ran through the edge of the city, was a rich source of gold. As in the American gold rush of 1849, people sought gold at Sardis. People came from far and near in their quest for gold.

"And unto the angel of the church in Sardis write; These things saith he that hath the seven Spirits of God, and the seven stars; I know thy works, that thou hast a name that thou livest, and art dead" (3:1).

The seven Spirits of God refer to the fullness of the Holy Spirit, as earlier discussed, and the seven stars are the seven angels of the seven churches. The church in Sardis had a great reputation but unfortunately did not have the character that backed up that reputation. If an outsider, a non-member had come into Sardis and inquired about the church, he would have gotten a good report. "It's a very active congregation. Why, the preacher's on fire. The elders are alive. The preacher is preaching, the deacons are 'deacing,' the elders are 'elding' and the congregation is congregating. Why that church is very much alive." It had that kind of reputation. In the society pages of the leading newspapers of Sardis, there was no doubt prominent mention of some of the members of the congregation. It was a church that had a reputation for living, but it was dead. Did you ever hear anyone speaking about another saying, "John is a fine man with certain splendid qualities," and then the word "but" comes in? That one little word makes all the difference. This is the type of church found in Sardis. It had a great reputation, but it was dead.

There are few things better organized than a cemetery, but there is no life there. Sadly this was the story of the church in Sardis with a name but no life.

It has been said of some people who are now 60 or 70 that they really died at 30 or 40 because they have not had a new idea in 30 years or entered any new ventures or experiences. The church in Sardis had all the appearance of being active and alive, a very productive and fruitful church. The Lord who really knew the church, however, knew that they were really dead. It is a tragedy when a church misrepresents itself to its neighbors, its community, its city. It is a tragedy when a Christian is not what he poses to be..

A tragedy of tragedies occurred in the church in Sardis. In a number of ways it was a dead church. I don't know all the ways it was a dead church, but I suspect that one of the ways was that it was a church living in the past. There are many churches like that today. They talk about the good old days. They talk about how good the preachers used to be. I take my hat off to all the preachers that are old and good and to all the churches that are old and good but not all that are good are old and not all that are old are good. We have to examine what's inside, the quality of it.

So our Lord told Sardis, **"Be watchful, and strengthen the things which remain, that are ready to die: for I have not found thy works perfect before God. Remember therefore how thou hast received and heard, and hold fast, and repent. If therefore thou shalt not watch, I will come on thee as a thief, and thou shalt not know what hour I will come upon thee"** (3:2-3).

When the Christians in ancient Sardis heard this verse, they remembered when Cyrus, the Persian king camped outside the city of Sardis, in 546 B.C. He camped there for months with no hope of coming inside the city because he could not breach the walls. With its strong walls, mostly natural walls, it seemed impregnable. One night, however, one of his soldiers keeping watch saw a soldier from Sardis coming down a narrow path between two parts of the wall.

He had come down to retrieve a fallen helmet. They informed Cyrus of the secret path, and at 3:00 in the morning the Persian army entered the city by the same pathway, each soldier walking single file up the path. When daylight broke on the city of Sardis, the Persian army had surrounded them. They had been so sure the Persians could not get in that they had not even posted a guard! So the Lord warned the Sardis Christians, "If therefore thou shalt not watch, I will come on thee as a thief, and thou shalt not know what hour I will come upon thee." Sardis had not watched in the critical hour. It was important that the Christians of Sardis not make the same mistake because the city of Sardis fell again in 214 B.C. to Antiochus the Great, in almost exactly the same way it fell to Cyrus!

"Thou hast a few names even in Sardis which have not defiled their garments; and they shall walk with me in white: for they are worthy. He that overcometh, the same shall be clothed in white raiment; and I will not blot out his name out of the book of life, but I will confess his name before my Father, and before his angels" (3:4-5).

White raiment was the special clothing of victory. They could look forward "to an inheritance incorruptible, and undefiled, and that fadeth not away, reserved in heaven" (1 Peter 1:4). The Lord promised the overcomer He would not blot his name out of the book of life. From Moses throughout the Bible, the book of life contains the names of those the Lord will eternally save. Moses spoke for Israel and said, "Yet now, if thou wilt forgive their sin–; and if not, blot me, I pray thee, out of thy book which thou hast written" (Exodus 32:32). Paul told the Philippians, "And I entreat thee also, true yokefellow, help those women which laboured with me in the gospel, with Clement also, and *with* other my fellowlabourers, whose names are in the book of life" (Philippians 4:3). Not only would their names remain in the book of life, but the Lord remembers those who overcome the world. **"He that hath an ear, let him hear what the Spirit saith unto the churches"** (3:6).

The city of Philadelphia was located about halfway between Sardis and Laodicea on one of the great international highways of the Roman Empire. Commerce from the East and from the West flowed along the highway that ran through the city of Philadelphia. The Roman armies marched up and down this highway conquering in the name of the mighty power of Rome. Eumenes, King of Pergamum, in the second century B.C., founded the city and named it in honor of his brother Attalus, whose loyalty had earned him the title, Philadelphus. It served as a great outpost of the Greco-Roman civilization in the Far East. It was strategically located in the valley of the Cogamus River, in an area subject to frequent earthquakes. Philadelphia was a great city with open doors for the spread of Greco-Roman civilization or any other ideas it wished to spread.

Of the seven letters, only Philadelphia and Smyrna received no condemnation. Smyrna had more commendation than Philadelphia, but Philadelphia was without rebuke. As in all the letters, the Lord describes and characterizes Himself in keeping with the condition of the church to whom he is writing.

"And to the angel of the church in Philadelphia write; These things saith he that is holy, he that is true, he that hath the key of David, he that openeth, and no man shutteth; and shutteth, and no man openeth" (3:7).

Let us imagine ourselves in Philadelphia in the year A.D. 95. A reader has risen to read this special letter to the church in Philadelphia as well as the rest of the book of Revelation. He tells us that He who is holy wrote the letter. In Leviticus, God said, "Sanctify yourselves therefore, and be ye holy: for I *am* the LORD your God" (20:7). Throughout the New Testament, the Lord Jesus Christ is the Holy One. The Jews criticized Him, but they could not find any real fault with Him. When He stood before Pontius Pilate in judgment, Pilate's verdict was, "I find no fault in this man" (Luke 23:4). Nineteen centuries of history have not reversed that verdict. We see then that the One writing the letter to the church in Philadelphia was unlike any other writer in the Roman Empire, being holy, without sin, without blemish. This is not true of the Roman emperors, senators and provincial governors who were unholy and sinful.

Not only is He holy, but He also is true. Throughout the Bible our Lord Jesus Christ and Almighty God are always true. The vision of chapter 19 portrays Christ as "Faithful and True." "I saw heaven opened, and behold a white horse; and he that sat upon him *was* called Faithful and True, and in righteousness he doth judge and make war" (Revelation 19:11). Jesus said, "I am the way, the truth, and the life: no man cometh unto the Father, but by me" (John 14:6).

This One who is true also has "the key of David." This indicates having authority in a very special way. His power and authority are indicated further in that He "openeth, and no man shutteth; and shutteth, and no man openeth."

"I know thy works" (3:8a).

The Lord does not enumerate these works as He did in the letter to the church in Ephesus, but since they received no condemnation, only commendation, the Philadelphia Christians were working Christians. If they had sung back then the hymns we now sing, without doubt they would have sung, 'To the work! To the work! We are servants of God." They would have repeated the words of the Lord, "I must work the works of him that sent me, while it is day: the night cometh, when no man can work" (John 9:4). Jesus also stated, "My Father worketh hitherto, and I work" (John 5:17). The church in Philadelphia was a beehive of activity, a congregation tremendously engaged in the work of the Lord.

"Behold, I have set before thee an open door, and no man can shut it: for thou hast a little strength, and hast kept my word, and hast not denied my name" (3:8b).

The word "door" in the Old and New Testaments indicates opportunity. Paul and Barnabas reported to the church in Antioch about their efforts in Galatia, "And when they were come, and had gathered the church together, they rehearsed all that God had done with them, and how he had opened the door of faith unto the Gentiles" (Acts 14:27). Paul said, "When I came to Troas to *preach* Christ's gospel, and a door was opened unto me of the Lord" (2 Corinthians 2:12). Paul also wrote, "I will tarry at Ephesus until Pentecost. For a great door and effectual is opened unto me, and *there are* many adversaries" (1 Corinthians 16:8-9). Looking back to the book of Esther, as Mordecai approached his kinswoman, queen of Persia, he said, "Think not with thyself that thou shalt escape in the king's house, more than all the Jews. For if thou altogether holdest thy peace at this time, *then* shall there enlargement and deliverance arise to the Jews from another place; but thou and thy father's house shall be destroyed: and who knoweth whether thou art come to the kingdom for *such* a time as this?" (Esther 4:13-14). Esther had a door of opportunity, just as the church in Philadelphia did.

Just as the church in Philadelphia had a great door of opportunity open, the same is true of churches today. We are living in great times. I know of no time this side of the New Testament that has more opportunity for the kingdom of God than these times in which we live. Many doors are open. We have many opportunities. We can accomplish immeasurable good for the cause of Christ.

"Behold, I will make them of the synagogue of Satan, which say they are Jews, and are not, but do lie; behold, I will make them to come and worship before thy feet, and to know that I have loved thee" (3:9).

The strongest opponents to Christianity in the first centuries of the history of the church were the Jews. Many of them claimed to be friends of God, but in reality they were the synagogue of Satan because the devil used them to persecute Christians.

"Because thou hast kept the word of my patience, I also will keep thee from the hour of temptation, which shall come upon all the world, to try them that dwell upon the earth" (3:10).

No doubt the Lord here speaks of the severe and killing persecution being waged by Domitian, the current Roman emperor, and by those who would succeed him. A great trial of persecution against Christians spread upon the whole world. The Lord would keep the Philadelphian Christians from it.

"Behold, I come quickly: hold that fast which thou hast, that no man take thy crown. Him that overcometh will I make a pillar in the temple of my God, and he shall go no more out: and I will write upon him the name of my God, and the name of the city of my God, *which is* **new Jerusalem, which cometh down out of heaven from my God: and** *I will write upon him* **my new name"** (3:11-12).

As the Lord promises to come quickly, we need to remember that in the New Testament there are many comings of the Lord. We often refer to the second coming, but it would be more accurate to refer to the final coming of our Lord. The Lord promised to come quickly in spirit to the Philadelphian Christians. Every letter closes with a promise to the overcomer. The promise here is that the overcomer will have a pillar in the temple of God. He will go in and out unharmed, and he will have written upon him the name of God and the name of the new Jerusalem that comes down from heaven and the name of Jesus Christ. These names indicate that the overcomer is blessed with belonging. What a tremendous possession he has in God and in the Lord Jesus Christ.

"He that hath an ear, let him hear what the Spirit saith unto the churches" (3:13). Every letter closes with this admonition.

Throughout the New Testament we see this admonition repeated. As our Lord closed the Sermon on the Mount, He said, "Therefore whosoever heareth these sayings of mine, and doeth them, I will liken him unto a wise man, which built his house upon a rock: And the rain descended, and the floods came, and the winds blew, and beat upon that house; and it fell not: for it was founded upon a rock. And every one that heareth these sayings of mine, and doeth them not, shall be likened unto a foolish man, which built his house upon the sand: And the rain descended, and the floods came, and the winds blew, and beat upon that house; and it fell: and great was the fall of it" (Matthew 7:24-27). In the parable of the soils, Jesus emphasized that we must be good soil. As the gospel is preached, there is just as much responsibility to hear as good soil as there is for the preacher to preach the truth in love.

Laodicea was a very wealthy city, an important banking center. Cicero, the great Roman statesman, did his chief banking in Laodicea. It was also a great manufacturing center. Eye salve was one of the main products made there. It was no mean city, but one of the great cities of the empire.

"And unto the angel of the church of the Laodiceans write; These things saith the Amen, the faithful and true witness, the beginning of the creation of God" (3:14).

The word "amen" literally means "may it be so." Christ is the faithful and true witness. He testified before Pontius Pilate and others faithfully and truthfully. Paul told Timothy, "The things that thou hast heard of me among many witnesses, the same commit thou to faithful men, who shall be able to teach others also" (2 Timothy 2:2). Among the Christians of the first century were those who were unfaithful, however. They did not testify to the reality of the deity of Jesus Christ but rather compromised and confessed the Roman emperor to be Lord and God.

Christ spoke as "the beginning of the creation of God." We have noted already how everyone spoke of Rome being eternal, living on forever and ever, but it is Christ who was there at the beginning of

God's creation. He was present with the Father in the morning of time, before the morning stars sang together, and the hills clapped their hands for joy. Jesus said, "Verily, verily, I say unto you, Before Abraham was, I am" (John 8:58). When Jesus used the words, *ego eimi*, "I am," He was saying, "Before Abraham came into existence, I was already in existence." The Greek tense of the verb implies continuous action in the past, pointing to His eternal existence.

John began his gospel account with a majestic statement about Christ's eternality: "In the beginning was the Word, and the Word was with God, and the Word was God. The same was in the beginning with God. All things were made by him; and without him was not any thing made that was made" (John 1:1-3). So He who wrote to the Laodicean Christians was the Amen, the faithful and true witness, and He who joined God in the creation of mankind and the creation of the heavens and the earth and all of her beauties.

"I know thy works, that thou art neither cold nor hot: I would thou wert cold or hot. So then because thou art lukewarm, and neither cold nor hot, I will spue thee out of my mouth" (3:15-16). We do not see the works of Laodicea in actions but in attitudes. The Lord would prefer that they be either hot or cold, but being lukewarm is very sickening to the Lord. At Hierapolis, a few miles north of Laodicea, a stream makes its way rapidly down the side of the road. The stream gushes out of Hierapolis and makes its way to Laodicea and beyond as it has for centuries. If anyone drinks this water, he becomes deathly sick at his stomach. The lukewarm water would cause 99 out of 100 to vomit. The church in Laodicea was a lukewarm church that made the Lord sick.

The members of the church in Laodicea were not cold so far as the work of the Lord; neither were they hot; neither were they up and doing. They were indifferent. The great prophet Amos warned those who came to Bethel to worship, "Woe to them *that are* at ease in Zion" (Amos 6:1). The people at Bethel were sitting upon their ivory couches. They were letting the rest of the world go by. They were taking things very easily. In your dating years, did you ever go out with a young woman or a young man who was lukewarm? They were totally unconcerned, totally indifferent. You didn't know if they appreciated you or not. When you got home from the date you may have confided in a brother or sister, "I just don't know how

Bill felt. I don't know if he is interested in me or not. He was so indifferent, so lukewarm." That is a condition that is very bad. I know that you prefer someone to be either cold to you or to be hot to you instead of being lukewarm.

Unfortunately, there are many lukewarm Christians. They don't really care what the church does. They aren't concerned about the decisions of the elders, about the sermons of the preacher, about the songs selected by the song director. They are an unconcerned congregation. They like to sit on the back seat, not the front. They don't like to be in the "Amen corner" because that commits them to involvement. They like to be uncommitted, unattached. Many times people reared in the country are faithful in attending church until they move into a big city where no one knows them. Then they may become lukewarm, unconcerned and unfaithful. Lukewarm members don't care if they attend church or not. They don't care what the church does. They want to be left alone in the crowd. They don't want the elders or the preacher or other members of the church to check on them. The situation of the church in Laodicea was tragic for its lukewarmness.

As bad as their lukewarmness was, there were even more problems in Laodicea. **"Because thou sayest, I am rich, and increased with goods, and have need of nothing; and knowest not that thou art wretched, and miserable, and poor, and blind, and naked"** (3:17), the Lord had to deal with them. They were not only lukewarm but they also thought they didn't need anything spiritually. They were satisfied. Their attitude was, "We have arrived! There is nothing else for us to do."

I heard of a church in Middle Tennessee that had virtually every seat filled, with chairs in the aisles and around the pulpit. A new member who moved in suggested a gospel meeting to the elders. They were not interested. They said, "Every seat is already full. Where would we put anyone else?" They were completely satisfied. There are many people like that. They have a little Bible knowledge, and they are completely satisfied with that little bit. They are satisfied with their prayer life, with their church attendance, with their church activities. That is a pathetic condition. There are preachers who are satisfied with their preparation for preaching. When preachers or Bible teachers or doctors or lawyers or song leaders or elders get satisfied with themselves, they are in a bad condition, especially if they are satisfied with their spiritual lives.

The Lord's prescription for Laodicea was clear: **" I counsel thee to buy of me gold tried in the fire, that thou mayest be rich; and white raiment, that thou mayest be clothed, and *that* the shame of thy nakedness do not appear; and anoint thine eyes with eyesalve, that thou mayest see"** (3:18). They had gold in the bank, but it was not the true, tested spiritual gold. They might have the eye salve from their factories, but it was not sufficient to cure their self-satisfied spiritual lives. They needed spiritual eye salve to cleanse their hearts and lives.

"As many as I love, I rebuke and chasten: be zealous therefore, and repent" (3:19). Being reproved and chastened is an indication that God loves us. When chastened in the crucible of faith, in the experiences of life and in the trials as they come, we realize how important it is to be faithful to God.

"Behold, I stand at the door, and knock: if any man hear my voice, and open the door, I will come in to him, and will sup with him, and he with me" (3:20). Most of us have seen the painting of Christ standing at the door of the human heart, with a lantern in his hand, and with his hair wet with the dew of the night. He knocks away at the door of that heart. He says, "I am standing at your door and knocking, and if you will just open I will come in and sup with you." Upon seeing that picture, a visitor said the artist had made a mistake. He had noticed that there is no knob on the outside of the door. There was no mistake, though, because the knob is on the inside. So it is with my heart and your heart. Christ will not force entrance. We control whether the door opens.

Finally, the Lord says, **"To him that overcometh will I grant to sit with me in my throne, even as I also overcame, and am set down with my Father in his throne. He that hath an ear, let him hear what the Spirit saith unto the churches"** (3:21-22).

What greater privilege could we conceive of than sitting down with the Lord Jesus on the throne of God in heaven itself? We can join with Christ himself, seated on David's throne since his ascension through the trackless blue of heaven as the wondering disciples looked on.

CHAPTER 4

DOXOLOGY BEFORE THE THRONE OF GOD AND VICTORY OVER PERSECUTION

Revelation 4-6

As we leave the study of the letters to the seven churches, we set the stage for chapter four by returning to the first chapter for John's commission to write. "Write the things which thou hast seen, and the things which are, and the things which shall be hereafter" (1:19). The events of chapters two and three are "the things which are," and as we continue in chapter four we shall see "the things which are, and the things which shall be hereafter."

We are still in western Asia Minor in one of these congregations, and we have experienced difficulties day after day, week after week and month after month. Our fellow laborers, our neighbors, our relatives and our friends who are not Christians have told us repeatedly of the power of the mighty Roman Empire. They have preached to us that it is an empire stretching from the Danube in the north to the Tropic of Cancer in the south and all the way from the Euphrates in the east to Spain in the west, the mightiest empire the world has ever known. They have told us that it has conquered every nation under the sun (except the Parthians), and its armies have marched over the Roman roads to victory after victory.

But now we Christians see something quite different. The Roman emperors no longer sit on their thrones. They sleep in the solemn silence of endless dust. The Roman Senate meets no more. The governors of the large Roman provinces have gone. Rome is gone along with all the other mighty nations that have forgotten God. Almighty God sits upon His throne, ruling the universe. This is the message of Revelation 4, that God is on His throne in all His omniscience, omnipresence and omnipotence. He rules with all authority as He has since before time began.

"**After this I looked, and, behold, a door *was* opened in heaven: and the first voice which I heard *was* as it were of a trumpet talking with me; which said, Come up hither, and I will show thee things which must be hereafter**" (4:1).

"After this" and "behold" remind us that something new and startling is being revealed. As noted in the discussion of the letter to the church in Philadelphia, the open door indicates a great opportunity to see into heaven itself. The voice that John heard was not a trumpet but sounded like a trumpet.

"**And immediately I was in the spirit; and, behold, a throne was set in heaven, and *one* sat on the throne. And he that sat was to look upon like a jasper and a sardine stone: and *there was* a rainbow round about the throne, in sight like unto an emerald**" (4:2-3).

No inhabitant of the Roman domain had ever beheld anything comparable in majesty, beauty or power to what John was able to see. God transported these Christians, many of whom were discouraged, spiritually to realms beyond where they did not see the realities of temporal Rome but the realities of the throne of God. The vision reveals the throne of God with the most beautiful and precious jewels.

"**And round about the throne *were* four and twenty seats: and upon the seats I saw four and twenty elders sitting, clothed in white raiment; and they had on their heads crowns of gold**" (4:4). These 24 elders show the universality of the dominion of God. Twenty-four is the perfect number 12 doubled. The 24 elders are the 12 patriarchs, the sons of Jacob of Old Testament times, and the 12 apostles of the Lamb, who were His ambassadors to the end of the earth. Crowned in eternity, they will bow before the throne of God.

"**And out of the throne proceeded lightnings and thunderings and voices: and *there were* seven lamps of fire burning before the throne, which are the seven Spirits of God**" (4:5).

The lightnings and thunderings and voices all demonstrate the tremendous power emanating from the throne of Almighty God. The seven lamps of fire as the seven Spirits of God demonstrate the fullness of God's power, a fullness demonstrated throughout the vision of the throne.

"And before the throne *there was* **a sea of glass like unto crystal: and in the midst of the throne, and round about the throne,** *were* **four beasts full of eyes before and behind. And the first beast** *was* **like a lion, and the second beast like a calf, and the third beast had a face as a man, and the fourth beast** *was* **like a flying eagle. And the four beasts had each of them six wings about** *him;* **and** *they were* **full of eyes within: and they rest not day and night, saying, Holy, holy, holy, Lord God Almighty, which was, and is, and is to come"** (4:6-8).

The sea of glass like crystal reflects and magnifies the glorious scene. The 24 elders are around the throne along with four fantastic creatures representing all creation. The first creature is the chief beast of the forest, the lion. A lion represents power. The second creature, like a calf, represents the domesticated animals. The third creature, with a face as a man, represents all mankind. The fourth creature, the flying eagle, represents the great outer spaces of the earth.

The picture is a powerful one. God Almighty sits on His throne surrounded by the faithful of all time in the 12 patriarchs and the 12 apostles as well as all creation bowed before him. This picture presents the persecuted Christians of Asia Minor with the reality of eternity, an eternity that will break again into time and deal with men upon the earth.

These creatures around the throne of God say unceasingly, "Holy, holy, holy, Lord God Almighty, which was, and is, and is to come." How assuring, how comforting was this great message from eternity to the children of God.

"And when those beasts give glory and honour and thanks to him that sat on the throne, who liveth for ever and ever, The four and twenty elders fall down before him that sat on the throne, and worship him that liveth for ever and ever, and cast their crowns before the throne, saying, Thou art worthy, O Lord, to receive glory and honour and power: for thou hast created all things, and for thy pleasure they are and were created" (4:9-11).

The 24 elders and the four creatures join to bow before the throne of Almighty God, Who is worthy to receive all the acclamation man can give. The Christians, forced to endure ceremonies to worship the Roman emperor, would understand that the Roman worship was nothing compared to the worship accorded God in heaven. The great Creator continues to rule. The great doxology before His throne offers Him the proper honor.

Oh, what a tremendous experience it would have been for you and me and all the children of God of all ages to sit with the Christians of Asia Minor and to hear these words and see these scenes. It would assure them again that they were part of the greatest cause that heaven or earth has ever known. The had assurance that the cause they were living for and risking their lives for would be triumphant. They had this assurance: "The kingdoms of this world are become *the kingdoms* of our Lord, and of his Christ; and he shall reign for ever and ever" (Revelation 11:15).

Revelation 4 presents the majesty, the omnipresence and the omniscience of God, the God who is really the One in control of human affairs and divine affairs, Who sits upon His throne in heaven, and who is really the One ruling the world and not the Caesars on the imperial thrones of Rome. Revelation 4 describes doxologies to Almighty God. This was very reassuring, comforting and meaningful to the Christians in these seven churches who received the book of Revelation.

Now chapter five concerns itself with doxologies to the Lord Jesus Christ, to His exaltation above all others being worshiped in the Roman Empire.

"And I [John] saw in the right hand of him that sat on the throne a book written within and on the backside, sealed with seven seals" (5:1).

Now the One seated upon the throne was Almighty God. The book was a scroll because codices had scarcely come into use at this time, and what we refer to as "a book" was a rolled-up parchment. A separate parchment was sealed with a seal, which would indicate that no one could open it except the one who had authority to open it. The Romans were great on seals, great on sealing documents, particularly important documents. Dipping back into Israel's history to Old Testament times, we also find this practice. We read in the books of Ezekiel and Isaiah and Daniel concerning scrolls sealed with seals, to be opened only by those who had authority.

"And I [John] saw a strong angel proclaiming with a loud voice, Who is worthy to open the book, and to loose the seals thereof?" By that he meant, "Who has the authority? Who's qualified to open these seals and these scrolls?" "No man in heaven, nor in earth, neither under the earth, was able to open the book neither to look thereon" (5:2-3). In other words, the angels searched heaven and earth and Hades for someone qualified to open this sealed scroll, and no one was qualified. And John "wept much, because no man was found worthy to open and to read the book, neither to look thereon" (5:4). Evidently John wept because the scrolls contained the redemptive plans of God for mankind until the Saturday evening of time; and if no one opened the scrolls, these plans would remain unknown.

"And one of the elders saith unto me, Weep not; behold, the Lion of the tribe of Juda, the Root of David, hath prevailed to open the book and to loose the seven seals thereof" (5:5). This is none other than the Lord Jesus Christ.

"And I beheld, and, lo, in the midst of the throne and of the four beasts, and in the midst of the elders, stood a Lamb as it had been slain, having seven horns and seven eyes, which are the seven Spirits of God, sent forth into all the earth" (5:6). The book of Revelation describes Our Lord as the Lamb of God numerous times. In Isaiah 53, Isaiah predicted that this Lamb would be led as to the slaughter and that He would not open His mouth but that He would submit to the great sacrifice. Concerning these seven horns, horns in the Old Testament signified power, and the seven eyes indicated omniscience. They are the seven Spirits of God, the seven characteristics of God which go forth into all the world.

"And he came and he took the book out of the right hand of him that sat on the throne. And when he had taken the book, the four beasts and the four *and* twenty elders fell down before the Lamb, having every one of them harps, and golden vials full of incense, which are the prayers of saints" (5:7-8). The 24 elders, whom we met first in Revelation 4, represent the 12 patriarchs of Israel and the 12 apostles of the Lamb. Having harps is a figure of speech because these creatures — the lion, and the calf, and the flying eagle, and the creature that had the face of a man — we can hardly conceive of us having and playing literal harps.

"And they sung a new song" (5:9a).

It was a song of redemption, not the song of Moses but the song of the Lamb. Revelation 14:3 tells about this new song of redemption. The book of Psalms refers to it prophetically a number of times.

"Thou art worthy to take the book and to open the seals thereof: for thou wast slain and hast redeemed us to God by the blood out of every kindred, and tongue, and people, and nation; and hast made us unto our God kings and priests: and we shall reign on the earth" (5:9b-10).

Reigning on the earth meant they lived in such a manner that their lives were reigning and were supreme among the sons of men.

"And I beheld, and I heard the voice of many angels round about the throne and the beasts and the elders: and the number of them was ten thousand times ten thousand, and thousands of thousands; saying with a loud voice, Worthy is the Lamb that was slain to receive power, and riches, and wisdom, and strength, and honour, and glory, and blessing. And every creature which is in heaven and on the earth and under the earth, and such as are in the sea, and all that are in them, heard I saying, Blessing, and honour and glory, and power, be unto him that sitteth upon the throne, and unto the Lamb for ever and ever. And the four beasts said, Amen. And the four *and* twenty elders fell down and worshiped him that liveth for ever and ever" (5:11-14).

Revelation 5 presented to the Christians of the seven churches a tremendously victorious scene, a scene beyond earth and sky. It was a scene that transpired in heaven itself where the Lord Jesus Christ received adoration and power and glory. It was such superior and surpassing adoration and power and glory that the triumphs of the Caesars as they marched from battlefields in victory on white horses, carrying their loot and their conquests behind them, cannot compare with it.

In Revelation 6 we begin the opening of the seven seals. "And I saw when the Lamb opened one of the seals, and I heard, as it were, the noise of thunder, and one of the four beasts saying, Come and see. And I saw and, behold: a white horse: and he that sat thereon had a bow; and a crown was given unto him: and he went forth conquering, and to conquer" (6:1-2).

The One who sat on the white horse was none other than the Lord Jesus Christ. A white horse is always symbolic of victory. The Roman generals always rode on white horses when they came home from battlefields where they had fought other peoples. But it refers here to the Lord Jesus Christ, Who has gone forth with His spiritual armies conquering and to conquer. He has come forth with a bow in His hand and with a crown given to Him. The bow suggests the Parthians and the Parthian army who fought on horses. The Romans were not able to fight on horses. They never learned cavalry work, but the Parthians did and were often victorious.

"And when he had opened the second seal, I heard the second beast say, Come and see. And there went out another horse *that was* **red: and** *power* **was given to him that sat thereon to take peace from the earth, and that they should kill one another: and there was given unto him a great sword"** (6:3-4).

Red is symbolic, at least in circumstances like these, of bloodshed, conflict and warfare. The record says that the rider of the red horse had power to take peace from the earth, which would seem to indicate civil war in the Roman Empire. There were in fact civil wars at this time.

"And when he had opened the third seal, I heard the third beast say, Come and see. And I beheld, and lo a black horse; and he that sat on him had a pair of balances in his hand" (6:5).

A black horse was symbolic of death. Death always characterizes war. A pair of balances in the hand of the one riding upon the black horse is indicative of when the battles close, when the victory is secure, when everything is counted and weighed up in the scales. We're not always sure who has won until the smoke of battle has cleared.

"And I heard a voice in the midst of the four beasts say, A measure of wheat for a penny, and three measures of barley for a penny; and *see* **thou hurt not the oil and the wine"** (6:6).

A measure of wheat for a denarius or a penny represented the pay for a complete day's work by a man. The three measures of barley, inasmuch as barley was less expensive than wheat, indicated the same. "Hurt not the oil and the wine." The oil and the wine in the empire of Rome were very lucrative products. We have an actual document stating that Domitian, the contemporary emperor, issued a decree to trim the vineyards in the provinces and destroy some of them, but he preserved the vineyards in Italy. So there goes forth this decree: "Don't hurt the oil and the wine."

"And when he had opened the fourth seal, I heard the voice of the fourth beast say, Come and see. And I looked, and behold, a pale horse: and his name that sat upon him, was Death; and Hell followed with him. And power was given unto them over the fourth part of the earth, to kill with sword, and with hunger, and with death, and with the beasts of the earth" (6:7-8).

The fourth part of the earth could represent the Parthian power.

"And when he had opened the fifth seal, I saw under the altar the souls of them that were slain for the word of God, and for the testimony which they held: And they cried with a loud voice, saying, How long, O Lord, holy and true, dost thou not judge and avenge our blood on them that dwell on the earth? And white robes were given unto every one of them; and it was said unto them that they should rest yet for a little season, until their fellowservants also and their brethren, that should be killed as they *were***, should be fulfilled"** (6:9-11).

There comes to the surface here in these three verses the theme, the great thrust of the book of Revelation. We have stressed that persecution was prevalent, inflicted upon the people of God throughout the vast Roman domain. These had lost their lives by the means of persecution. Some lives were extinguished by the jaws of lions and some by the flames of stakes, but nevertheless, they were under the altar of God and they were crying out, "How long, O Lord, how long must this go on?" The twentieth chapter of the book of Revelation in the fourth verse answers their question. "And I saw thrones, and they sat upon them, and judgment was given unto them: and *I saw* the souls of them that were beheaded for the witness of Jesus, and for the word of God, and which had not worshiped the beast, neither his image, neither had received *his* mark upon their foreheads, or in their hands; and they lived and reigned with Christ a thousand years." White robes being given unto them meant robes of victory.

"And I beheld when he had opened the sixth seal, and lo there was a great earthquake; and the sun became black as sackcloth of hair, and the moon became as blood; and the stars of heaven fell unto the earth, even as a fig tree casteth her untimely figs,

when she is shaken of a mighty wind. And the heaven departed as a scroll when it is rolled together; and every mountain and island were moved out of their places. And the kings of the earth, and the great men, and the rich men and the chief captains, and the mighty men, and every bondman and every free man, hid themselves in the dens and in the rocks of the mountains; and said to the mountains and to the rocks, Fall on us, and hide us from the face of him that sitteth on the throne, and from the wrath of the Lamb: for the great day of their wrath is come; and who is able to stand?" (6:12-17).

This sixth seal, as God revealed it unto John and to the Christians of the seven churches of western Asia Minor, was a seal that indicated a great catastrophe in nature. It may refer to the eruption of Mount Vesuvius and the destruction of close-by cities like Pompeii. There is also some reference to the end of the world when the sun shall turn into darkness and the moon shall turn into blood.

This scroll had seven seals, and as seal after seal was broken, that part of the scroll was unrolled and the message of that part of the scroll was given. God here is making known to His people what is going on, but which the eyes of the Roman people and the eyes of many members of the Roman government do not see. These affairs are really occurring in heaven itself. There God rules; there is where we find what really counts. Here we have expressions of the fact that God is in His heaven. Not everything is right with the world, but God is in the saddle and is upon the throne. He will right everything. The Old Testament and the New Testament join each other in abundantly testifying to this reality. We must bear in mind that God always has the last word. He operates in the hearts of men where we make proposals and He makes disposals. His will is final. That's what Revelation 6 is saying to us.

The horses that John saw, we understand were not literal horses but were symbolic of the fact that they are creatures used by Almighty God in a figurative way, in ways that will bring the message of God to the people of God most effectively. They cannot be literal horses. There are those who take the harps as literal harps and say if there are harps in heaven, there must be harps in the church. At least, what's good enough for heaven should be good enough for the church. But that does not follow. Babies are in heaven, but babies are not members of the church. If you're going to put a literal harp in the worship of the church because the sound like unto a harp is employed in the book of Revelation as referring to heaven, then you must put horses in the church, too. If the preacher decides to ride through the doors on a white horse on Sunday morning and come right down the aisle into the pulpit, we cannot forbid him if we're going to say that because there may be some kind of harp in heaven, it should be in the church. It just doesn't follow.

CHAPTER 5

THE 144,000

Revelation 7

Revelation 7 presents an interval, a let up of the seven seals. Six of them have been given. We are waiting for the seventh. **"And after these things"** (a Greek expression used in the book of Revelation to introduce a new topic, or a new line of thought), John **"saw four angels standing on the four corners of the earth, holding the four winds of the earth, that the wind should not blow on the earth, nor on the sea, nor on any tree"** (7:1). If you would use a concordance, you would see that the word "angel" occurs more than 100 times in Revelation. The book, as we have pointed out to you, is apocalyptic literature. In such literature, angelology abounds. Angels are instruments of God. The word *angelos*, the Greek noun translated "angel," is from the Greek verb *angello* that means to send with a commission. The other Greek verb is *pempo* that signifies just to send, not necessarily with a commission, as a mother may send a child out into the yard. *Angelos* means that these creatures were missionaries and messengers of God.

John saw four angels standing on the four corners of the earth. In other years, some used this statement as proof that the earth is flat, for how can the earth have four corners unless it is flat? Again, we must not take this literally. We take it relatively. While the earth does not have four corners, there are four points of the compass. The angels were holding the four winds of the earth, the winds of the north and the south, of the east and the west, that they should not blow on the earth or the sea or any tree.

"And I saw another angel ascending from the east, having the seal of the living God: and he cried with a loud voice to the four angels, to whom it was given to hurt the earth and the sea, Saying, Hurt not the earth, neither the sea, nor the trees, till we have sealed the servants of our God in their foreheads" (7:2-3).

Sealing was a great practice in the Roman Empire throughout her provinces. Sealing something indicates belonging to the one who has sealed it. This angel ascending from the sunrise has the seal of the living God to seal the children of God and the command for no wind to blow on the earth or sea or tree until God has sealed His servants in their foreheads to indicate they were His children and His servants. In Egypt all the followers of Dionysius had the Dionysian seal indicating they belonged to that cult. Such was true throughout the vast Roman Empire. The children of God had the seal of God, indicating they belonged to Him and not to Caesar.

"And I heard the number of them which were sealed, *and there were* **sealed an hundred and forty** *and* **four thousand of all the tribes of the children of Israel"** (7:4).

Of the tribe of Judah 12,000, of Reuben 12,000, of Gad 12,000, of Asher 12,000, and Naphtali, Manasseh, Simeon, Levi, Issachar, Zebulun and Joseph and Benjamin each 12,000, totaling 144,000 (7:5-8). The list omits the tribe of Dan. Students of the book of Revelation have wondered why. My persuasion is that God omitted the Danites because in the tribe of Dan calf worship originated. The tribe of Dan began apostasy from the worship of Jehovah. Also, it was the belief of some that among the people from the tribe of Dan the anti-Christ would arise. Therefore Dan is omitted.

The 144,000 is not a literal number as Jehovah's Witnesses may claim. The 144,000 are not the only ones saved, by a tremendous margin, as we learn later in the chapter. The 144,000 are representative of all the saved of Old Testament times. Here between the sixth and seventh seals these 144,000 of Old Testament days come to the surface, and God numbers them with the saved at the end of time as well as before the end of time.

"After this I beheld, and, lo, a great multitude, which no man could number, of all nations, and kindreds, and people, and tongues, stood before the throne, and before the Lamb, clothed with white robes, and palms in their hands" (7:9).

An *innumerable* number suggests so many that the sands of the sea do not compare with them, and the stars of the heavens do not relate to them. They were countless. They had white robes that were emblematic of victory. They had overcome. In Revelation 2 and 3 a promise was always to the overcomer. They had palms in their hands representing victory. You remember when Jesus rode in triumph into Jerusalem on a Lord's Day morning. The people went out to meet Him with palms in their hands, emblematic of the approaching victory, as they conceived of their Messiah.

"And cried with a loud voice, saying, Salvation to our God which sitteth upon the throne, and unto the Lamb" (7:10).

Here is a message from heaven that says salvation is *not* from the Roman powers. The Roman people at this time had come to say, "Give us more circuses and hand us out more food. We're looking to Rome as our Saviour, temporally and otherwise." But it is not Rome who will save. It is God and His Son Who shed His blood on Calvary for the salvation of the world.

"And all the angels stood round about the throne, and *about* the elders and the four beasts, and fell before the throne on their faces, and worshiped God" (7:11). They did not worship in the imperial temples around the empire. They did not worship the Roman emperor or his image, but they were worshiping Almighty God, and in this worship they were saying, "Amen," "may it be so."

"Blessing, and glory, and wisdom, and thanksgiving and honour, and power, and might, *be* unto our God for ever and ever. Amen" (7:12).

Remember Daniel 2:44: "And in the days of these kings shall the God of heaven set up a kingdom, which shall never be destroyed: and the kingdom shall not be left to other people, *but* it shall break in pieces and consume all these kingdoms, and it shall stand for ever." In fulfillment of this prophecy in Daniel we read in Revelation 11:15 that the kingdoms of this world will become the kingdoms of our Lord and of His Christ. That is what is being said here when all the angels of glory, the 24 elders representing the people of Old and New Testament times, and the four living creatures representing all of creation bow down before Almighty God and offer this doxology, not to the imperial power of Rome, but to Almighty God who rules in the kingdoms of men as Daniel states.

"And one of the elders answered, saying unto me, What are these which are arrayed in white robes? and whence came they? And I said unto him, Sir, thou knowest. And he said to me, These are they which came out of great tribulation, and have washed their robes, and made them white in the blood of the Lamb" (7:13-14). The great tribulation referred to severe persecution. By obeying the gospel and thus contacting the blood of the Lamb, they had their sins washed away in the precious blood of the Lord Jesus Christ. His cleansing blood made them whole.

"Therefore are they before the throne of God; and they serve him day and night in his temple" (7:15a).

The decree that came from the imperial office in the city of Rome was that all in the empire had to worship the image of the Roman emperor at least once a year in some imperial temple. But the children of God serve God day and night incessantly throughout the months and the years of their lives until and beyond the end of time.

"And he that sitteth on the throne shall dwell among them. They shall hunger no more, neither thirst any more" (7:15b-16a). We read about this again in Revelation 21:3: "Behold, the tabernacle of God *is* with men, and he will dwell with them, and they shall be his people, and God himself shall be with them, *and be* their God." We shall walk and talk. My God and I shall go through the fields together.

"They shall hunger no more, neither thirst any more; neither shall the sun light on them, nor any heat. For the Lamb which is in the midst of the throne shall feed them, and shall lead them unto living fountains of waters: and God shall wipe away all tears from their eyes" (7:16-17).

This is a foretaste of what we read about in Revelation 21. Here in verse 15 we read that His servants shall serve Him day and night in His temple.

So we have the 144,000 and the white-robed multitude of every tongue and every people, of all the races of mankind since the beginning of time until the end of time, worshiping and serving Almighty God. One of the grandest things about heaven is that it will be a land where we will serve God. We'll serve Him day and night in His temple.

CHAPTER 6

THE SEVEN TRUMPETS
Revelation 8-9

"And when he had opened the seventh seal there was silence in heaven about the space of half an hour" (8:1).

When the sixth chapter closed with the opening of the sixth seal, there was an intermission somewhat, in which we see the 144,000 of the Old Testament days and the innumerable number of all time numbered among those saved eternally. Now after that break and after the opening of this sixth seal, we have the opening of the seventh and last seal. After its opening there was a silence in heaven "about the space of half an hour." There was no angel or elder speaking, no chorus of praise or statement of adoration. It was a silence in contrast to the opening of seals one, two, three, four, five and six, and what shall follow the opening of the seventh seal, the tumult that ensues.

Silence always indicates that something is to come. The silence here indicates the coming of a storm, a tremendous storm, in which God will visit His wrath and vengeance upon the Roman people. The silence was about a half an hour. This is not to be taken literally. It is a figure of speech indicating a short time. One of the great mistakes in studying the book of Revelation is to major in the minors and to minor in the majors and to try to make much out of very little, to try to read into it things that John did not have in mind. We're not going to take the space of about half an hour and spin a theological thread or so from it, but in accord with the symbolic character of the book it indicates a short period of time.

"**And I saw,**" that is John saw, "**the seven angels which stood before God; and to them were given seven trumpets**" (8:2).

These seven angels are different from the other seven angels of the book of Revelation, different from all the other angels of the book. These seven angels are the angels of presence, and the book of Tobit, one of the pseudepigraphical books, written between the Old and New Testaments, names these seven angels. Their names are Uriel, Raphael, Raguel, Michael, Sariel, Gabriel, and Remuel (Tobit 12:15). In Tobit 19:15 we also read, "I am Raphael, one of the seven holy angels who present prayers of the saints and go in before the glory of the holy one." While Zacharias, the father of John the Baptist, followed his course as a priest to offer sacrifice in the temple, a tremendously high privilege for him and other priests, Gabriel appeared unto him and said, "I am Gabriel that stands in the presence of God" (Luke 1:19). Since Gabriel describes himself as one who stands in the presence of God, we see these seven as angels of the presence of God, who stood in His presence and were very near to Him to serve as messengers for Him.

The record adds that there were given unto them seven trumpets. The New Testament pictures angels as men or as messengers with trumpets. A trumpet always announced something tremendously significant and usually something with an ill omen or punishment. According to Joshua 6:13, the priests went before the ark of the Lord blowing trumpets. In Joel 2:1 we read, "Blow ye the trumpet in Zion, and sound an alarm in my holy mountain." This suggests that this announcement, this blowing of the trumpet, meant something significant was coming.

Trumpets also indicate judgment. "And it shall come to pass in that day, *that* the great trumpet shall be blown, and they shall come which were ready to perish in the land of Assyria, and the outcasts in the land of Egypt, and shall worship the LORD in the holy mount at Jerusalem" (Isaiah 27:13). In 1 Corinthians 15:52 we read, "in a moment, in the twinkling of an eye, at the last trump." So a trumpet will announce the coming of our Lord according to 1 Corinthians 15:52 and 1 Thessalonians 4. The trumpet will announce the raising of the dead in cemeteries of all time throughout the world and in the mausoleums connected with these cemeteries as well as in the sea that has its graves holding the dead.

Verses three through five begin a new paragraph. **"And another angel came and stood at the altar, having a golden censer; and there was given unto him much incense, that he should offer** *it* **with the prayers of all saints upon the golden altar which was before the throne. And the smoke of the incense,** *which came* **with the prayers of the saints, ascended up before God out of the angel's hand. And the angel took the censer, and filled it with fire of the altar, and cast** *it* **into the earth: and there were voices, and thunderings, and lightnings, and an earthquake"** (8:3-5).

Incense connected with prayer always indicated a sweet savor going up to the nostrils of God. It usually signified that God would hear and answer the prayer. Fire being cast down upon the earth was indicative that punishment was coming. Our Lord referred to the fact that God would cast fire down upon the earth.

"And the seven angels which had the seven trumpets prepared themselves to sound. The first angel sounded, and there followed hail and fire mingled with blood, and they were cast upon the earth: and the third part of trees was burnt up, and all green grass was burnt up" (8:6-7).

Following hail and fire after the sounding of the first trumpet is reminiscent of one of the Egyptian plagues in the time of Moses. It also indicates punishment. The third part of the earth probably indicated the part of the Roman Empire that was adjacent to the Parthian Empire, which lay just east of the Euphrates River, the eastern boundary of the Roman Empire. The Parthians were the people whom the Romans had never been able to conquer because of their method of warfare as contrasted with that of the Romans.

"And the second angel sounded, and as it were a great mountain burning with fire was cast into the sea: and the third part of the sea became blood" (8:8). This is also reminiscent of another of the Egyptian plagues.

"And the third part of the creatures which were in the sea, and had life, died; and the third part of the ships were destroyed. And the third angel sounded, and there fell a great star from heaven, burning as it were a lamp, and it fell upon the third part of the rivers, and upon the fountains of waters; And the name of the star is called Wormwood: and the third part of the waters became wormwood; and many men died of the waters, be-

cause they were made bitter" (8:9-11). The word "wormwood" is
a translation of the Hebrew word that means "bitter," and signifies
punishment upon the enemies of God. If you are acquainted with
The Screwtape Letters written by the late C.S. Lewis, you will know
the use he made of "wormwood."

**"And the fourth angel sounded, and the third part of the sun
was smitten, and the third part of the moon, and the third part
of the stars; so as the third part of them was darkened, and the
day shone not for a third part of it, and the night likewise"** (8:12).

All persons who study the book of Revelation sanely know that
references to a third part of the sun and a third part of the stars are
not to be taken literally. If they were smitten, life would not be.
Planets would not exist. So what he said is symbolic of heaven, that
is the sky above us, and the earth beneath us and around us.
Symbolically they are going to share in the punishment God is going to visit upon those to whom vengeance belongs, as Paul quoted from the Old Testament in Romans 12.

**"And I beheld, and heard an angel flying through the midst
of heaven, saying with a loud voice, Woe, woe, woe, to the inhabiters of the earth by reason of the other voices of the trumpet of the three angels, which are yet to sound!"** (8:13).

Although the punishment had been severe to date, it is going to
be worse when these other three angels sound, indicating their punishment upon the enemies of God.

These 13 verses that constitute chapter 8 are all figurative, except
perhaps the first one, and it is in a sense. They unite in giving a message to the Christians of the seven churches who received the book
of Revelation. That message was the assurance that the cause for
which they were living and dying was a cause that would triumph
over Rome, that mighty empire, although men had said a thousand
times or more, "Rome is eternal and invincible, unconquerable."

**"And the fifth angel sounded, and I saw a star fall from heav-
en unto the earth: and to him was given the key of the bottomless pit"** (9:1).

Stars played a significant part, being instruments of God or messengers of God. Falling from heaven would suggest a direct message from God.

"And he opened the bottomless pit; and there arose a smoke out of the pit, as the smoke of a great furnace; and the sun and the air were darkened by reason of the smoke of the pit. And there came out of the smoke locusts upon the earth: and unto them was given power, as the scorpions of the earth have power" (9:2-3).

If you will look to S.R. Driver's commentary on the book of Joel in the *Cambridge Bible for Schools and Colleges*, you will find it rather illuminating as to the part played by locusts in the ancient world. These locusts are not the kind we see today but locusts larger and more devastating that would sweep across any portion of a land or country and destroy everything before them. In this case, locusts, with the power of scorpions, came out of the smoke and would sting. Some of their stings would cause pain that would last for five months; some even caused death.

"And it was commanded them that they should not hurt the grass of the earth, neither any green thing, neither any tree; but only those men which have not the seal of God in their foreheads" (9:4).

We are anticipating some, but let's return to chapter 7 where God sealed His servants with His own seal. Then, if we'll advance to chapter 13 we will learn that they who did not have the seal of the Roman emperor, the imperial stamp or mark, were those who could not buy or sell. The Roman authorities oftentimes killed them by the sword or by the lions or by burning them at the stake. But God exempts those who have His seal. Those who do not have the seal will be tormented for five months. "And to them it was given that they should not kill them, but that they should be tormented five months: and their torment *was* as the torment of a scorpion, when he striketh a man" (9:5).

"And in those days shall men seek death, and shall not find it; and shall desire to die, and death shall flee from them" (9:6).

The patriarch Job states in the great drama of the book of Job that there were those in his day who sought to die, but death fled from them. There are other passages in the Old Testament that state the same. So death was preferred to life here. Oftentimes that happens in the experiences of men and women here today. Some would rather die than live, because life is so miserable for them. These people in the Roman Empire who were going to suffer punishment and death preferred death as soon as possible.

"And the shapes of the locusts *were* like unto horses prepared unto battle; and on their heads *were* as it were crowns like gold, and their faces *were* as the faces of men" (9:7).

A large number of these locusts sweeping across the country produces a great humming and buzzing sound. Everybody knows that they leave complete destruction in their path.

"And they had hair as the hair of women, and their teeth were as *the teeth* of lions. And they had breastplates, as it were breastplates of iron; and the sound of their wings *was* as the sound of chariots of many horses running to battle. And they had tails like unto scorpions, and there were stings in their tails: and their power *was* to hurt men five months. And they had a king over them, *which is* the angel of the bottomless pit, whose name in the Hebrew tongue *is* Abaddon, but in the Greek tongue hath *his* name Apollyon" (9:8-11).

"Abaddon" occurs at least six times in the Old Testament. "Apollyon" was its Greek equivalent. Apollyon or Abaddon was the head of this great horde of locusts, this great number of scorpions who were punishing the enemies of God who did not have the seal of God upon them.

"One woe is past; *and,* behold, there come two woes more hereafter. And the sixth angel sounded, and I heard a voice from the four horns of the golden altar which is before God, Saying to the sixth angel which had the trumpet, Loose the four angels which are bound in the great river Euphrates. And the four angels were loosed, which were prepared for an hour, and a day, and a month, and a year, for to slay the third part of men. And the number of the army of the horsemen *were* two hundred thousand thousand: and I heard the number of them" (9:12-16).

This evidently refers to Parthian cavalrymen and the Parthian army. The Parthian soldiers fought upon horses. They charged forward with well-trained horses like the trained elephants of the Indian army. These horses also had fighting equipment worked into their tails and wrapped around them so that after they charged forward, they could charge, so to speak, backward. They would fight in warfare "going and coming." The Romans could not cope with this.

They were not trained to fight on horses. They were ineffective in warfare against the Parthians and did not feel equal to them.

"And thus I saw the horses in the vision, and them that sat on them, having breastplates of fire, and of jacinth, and brimstone: and the heads of the horses _were_ as the heads of lions; and out of their mouths issued fire and smoke and brimstone" (9:17). Of course, this is figurative but indicative of the fierceness with which the horses and those on them would fight.

"For their power is in their mouth, and in their tails: for their tails _were_ like unto serpents, and had heads, and with them they do hurt" (9:19). That is, their tails were weapons.

"And the rest of the men which were not killed by these plagues yet repented not of the works of their hands, that they should not worship devils, and idols of gold, and silver, and brass, and stone, and of wood: which neither can see, nor hear, nor walk: Neither repented they of their murders, nor of their sorceries, nor of their fornication, nor of their thefts" (9:20-21).

The reaction among the Parthians and probably the Romans or at least a segment of the Romans was negative. When they saw these expressions of the vengeance of God, it was not helpful to them, but it increased their antagonism. It made their lifestyle all the worse.

CHAPTER 7

THE LITTLE BOOK AND THE TWO WITNESSES

Revelation 10-11

"And I saw another mighty angel come down from heaven, clothed with a cloud: and a rainbow *was* upon his head, and his face *was* as it were the sun, and his feet as pillars of fire: And he had in his hand a little book open: and he set his right foot upon the sea, and *his* left *foot* on the earth" (10:1-2).

This reminds us of Revelation 5:1 where a little sealed book lay in the hand of God. John wanted to know its contents. When someone worthy to cut the seals and open the scroll was sought, only our Lord was worthy. This little book reminds us of an experience of the great prophet Ezekiel in ancient Babylon when Ezekiel "swallowed" the scroll (Ezekiel 3:1-2).

"And cried with a loud voice, as *when* a lion roareth: and when he had cried, seven thunders uttered their voices. And when the seven thunders had uttered their voices, I was about to write: and I heard a voice from heaven saying unto me, Seal up those things which the seven thunders uttered, and write them not" (10:3-4). This section is similar to the commands of God in the last part of Daniel. He saw visions to be sealed up, not to be revealed then. The revelation was waiting God's good time.

"And the angel which I saw stand upon the sea and upon the earth lifted up his hand to heaven, And sware by him that liveth for ever and ever, who created heaven, and the things that therein are, and the earth, and the things that therein are, and the sea, and the things which are therein, that there should be time no longer" (10:5-6).

While the American Standard Version renders the end of the verse, "There shall be delay no longer," the King James rendering, "There should be time no longer," is preferable. The meaning is that the delay in punishing the Roman people will be no longer; the time has come (see Revelation 14:7). The hour of judgment is come.

"But in the days of the voice of the seventh angel, when he shall begin to sound, the mystery of God should be finished, as he hath declared to his servants the prophets" (10:7).

The mystery of God was hidden for ages, even before time began, but Paul revealed the mystery in the reality that "God was in Christ reconciling the world to himself" (2 Corinthians 5:19).

"And the voice which I heard from heaven spake unto me again, and said, Go *and* take the little book which is open in the hand of the angel which standeth upon the sea and upon the earth. And I went unto the angel, and said unto him, Give me the little book. And he said unto me, Take *it,* and eat it up; and it shall make thy belly bitter, but it shall be in thy mouth sweet as honey" (10:8-9).

This is reminiscent of the experience of the prophet Ezekiel. God told him exactly what He told John. We do not take his eating a book literally but as a figure of speech. The meaning of it is that the message of the book is sweet as honey, but the reception that it received is as bitter and as negative as a reception could be. Many of the people among the Romans would receive the preaching of the gospel. Receptive hearts would accept it.

"And I took the little book out of the angel's hand, and ate it up; and it was in my mouth sweet as honey: and as soon as I had eaten it, my belly was bitter. And he said unto me," that is, the angel, **"Thou must prophesy again before many peoples, and nations, and tongues, and kings"** (10:10-11).

This means that John was yet to preach the gospel extensively over the Roman Empire, even though he was of a ripe old age already. It may mean that those he trained would carry the message that he'd given them in addition to what John had done. One of the church fathers tells that John the apostle had a school for preachers in the city of Ephesus. This is probable. He spent his last years there and was very active and productive in his work in ancient Ephesus.

"And there was given me a reed like unto a rod" (11:1a).

This builds upon the experience of Ezekiel who was given a reed as a measuring rod. A measuring rod primarily had two purposes: measuring for destruction if you were going to destroy a house or a building or measuring for construction. Anyone who would scientifically destroy this building or dismantle it would do it by measuring instruments. Those who built the building in other years did it by measuring means. So that's what is in mind here, that there is going to be a measuring, a judgment.

"And the angel stood, saying, Rise, and measure the temple of God [the Jerusalem temple] **and the altar, and them that worship therein. But the court which is without the temple leave out, and measure it not; for it is given unto the Gentiles: and the holy city shall they tread under foot forty** *and* **two months"** (11:1b-2).

Without doubt the holy city was Jerusalem. The record in Matthew 4 tells that the devil took Jesus unto the holy city. A number of times the New Testament refers to Jerusalem as the holy city. So it is the holy city here, and the holy city they shall tread. Who are the "they"? They are none other than the Romans, called here the *ethnos* in the Greek or "the nations." They zeroed in on Rome herself. The reference here is undoubtedly to the destruction of Jerusalem at the hands of the Romans under the commanding leadership of Titus, the son of Vespasian and the brother of Domitian.

"The holy city shall they tread under foot forty *and* two months." Forty-two months is exactly three and a half years. In the third part of the year A.D. 66, the Jewish-Roman War erupted in the city of Caesarea. Herod the Great built Caesarea on the Mediterranean Sea to honor Augustus Caesar. The war terminated three and a half years later in the destruction of Jerusalem.. As He looked at the temple in all of its magnificence Jesus said that the time was coming when not one stone would be left on another. That time came when the Romans destroyed Jerusalem completely. They had so many crosses on which to hang Jews they didn't have room to place the crosses around Jerusalem. Josephus' account of the destruction of Jerusalem reveals how terrible it was.

"And I will give *power* **unto my two witnesses, and they shall prophesy a thousand two hundred** *and* **threescore days, clothed in sackcloth"** (11:3).

That again is the time of the Jewish-Roman War. These two witnesses will be clothed in sackcloth, representing mourning. **"These are the two olive trees, and the two candlesticks standing before the God of the earth. And if any man will hurt them, fire proceedeth out of their mouth, and devoureth their enemies: and if any man will hurt them, he must in this manner be killed. These have power to shut heaven, that it rain not in the days of their prophecy: and have power over waters to turn them to blood, and to smite the earth with all plagues, as often as they will"** (11:4-6).

These two witnesses are Moses, who turned the water into blood, and Elijah, who by prayer closed the heavens so that it did not rain and by prayer opened the heavens so that it did rain. They are unmistakably Moses and Elijah.

"And when they shall have finished their testimony, the beast that ascendeth out of the bottomless pit shall make war against them, and shall overcome them, and kill them. And their dead bodies *shall lie* in the street of the great city, which spiritually is called Sodom and Egypt, where also our Lord was crucified" (11:7-8). The beast that comes up out of the bottomless pit, or abyss, is the Roman emperor. The Sibylline Oracles, one of the inter-testamental books, labels Jerusalem as Sodom at one time and also Egypt because of its corruption. It was morally and spiritually like Sodom and Egypt.

"And they of the people and kindreds and tongues and nations shall see their dead bodies three days and an half, and shall not suffer their dead bodies to be put in graves. And they that dwell upon the earth shall rejoice over them, and make merry, and shall send gifts one to another; because these two prophets tormented them that dwelt on the earth" (11:9-10).

A prophet often torments the people around him. Moses did that. So did Elijah. Their revelations from God were contrary to those that the people claimed to have and to the ways of life that they wanted to live.

"And after three days and a half the Spirit of life from God entered into them, and they stood upon their feet; and great fear fell upon them which saw them. And they heard a great voice from heaven saying unto them, Come up hither. And they as-

cended up to heaven in a cloud; and their enemies beheld them" (11:11-12).

Elijah ascended to heaven in a chariot. Moses went up to Mount Nebo, a very high mountain, and there he died. No man knows his grave even today.

"And the same hour was there a great earthquake, and the tenth part of the city fell, and in the earthquake were slain of men seven thousand: and the remnant were affrighted, and gave glory to the God of heaven" (11:13).

This probably refers to the final days and weeks of Jerusalem during the Jewish-Roman War.

"The second woe is past; *and,* **behold, the third woe cometh quickly. And the seventh angel sounded; and there were great voices in heaven, saying, The kingdoms of this world are become** *the kingdoms* **of our Lord, and of his Christ; and he shall reign for ever and ever"** (11:14-15).

We have said that this is the key verse of the entire book of Revelation. It is a fulfillment of a prophecy of Daniel given in the sixth century before Christ, recorded in Daniel 2:44: "And in the days of these kings shall the God of heaven set up a kingdom, which shall never be destroyed: and the kingdom shall not be left to other people, *but* it shall break in pieces and consume all these kingdoms, and it shall stand for ever." The prophecy referred to the emperors or kings of the Roman Empire. In the days of those kings neither Rome nor Greece nor Egypt will set up a kingdom, but the God of heaven will set it up. No man can destroy this kingdom set up by Him, and its rulership or sovereignty belongs to the people of God and God Himself. It will break in pieces all of these kingdoms. It will stand forever.

Teaching in Caesarea Philippi, Jesus said, "Upon this rock I will build my church; and the gates of hell shall not prevail against it" (Matthew 16:18). Although they crucified our Lord and placed a Roman seal upon His tomb, He burst the bars of death to come forth bringing life and immortality to light and established His church through the instrumentality of His apostles. While there is some immediate reference made to that, the primary thrust, the eternal thrust of the statement of our Lord to Peter was and is that the gates of Hades shall not prevail against the church of God and that she will march triumphantly on, making one conquest after another until her commander-in-chief places the flag of victory upon the hill of victory. The kingdoms of this world will become the kingdoms of our Lord and of His Christ, and every plant that our heavenly Father hath not planted will be rooted up. The writer in Hebrews 12:28 referred to the fact that the kingdom was an immovable kingdom. It was and is.

"And the four and twenty elders, which sat before God on their seats, fell upon their faces, and worshiped God, Saying, We give thee thanks, O Lord God Almighty, which art, and wast, and art to come; because thou hast taken to thee thy great power, and hast reigned" (11:16-17).

Again the scene shows the 24 elders, representing the completeness of the 12 tribes and the 12 apostles, the Old Covenant and the New, fall on their faces in worship to God, Who is worthy of worship because of His omnipotence and eternality. Rome will fall, along with all the other nations that forget God. God reigns always.

"And the nations were angry, and thy wrath is come, and the time of the dead, that they should be judged, and that thou shouldest give reward unto thy servants the prophets, and to the saints, and them that fear thy name, small and great; and shouldest destroy them which destroy the earth" (11:18).

The victory of the church provoked the anger of the nations.

"And the temple of God was opened in heaven, and there was seen in his temple the ark of his testament: and there were lightnings, and voices, and thunderings, and an earthquake, and great hail" (11:19).

Opening the temple of God in heaven revealed the ark of the covenant. The ark indicated the presence of God in the temple and here shows God's continued presence within His church. Those first century Christians remembered our Lord's promise in Matthew 28:20, "Lo, I am with you alway, *even* unto the end of the world."

CHAPTER 8

DESTINY IN THE BALANCE

Revelation 12

Chapter 12 concerns itself with the great confrontation between the church and the empire, between God and the devil, between Christ and the Caesars, between monotheism and polytheism, and for everything that was right against everything that was wrong.

"And there appeared a great wonder [or sign] **in heaven"** (12:1a). In his gospel account John stated, "And many other signs truly did Jesus in the presence of his disciples, which are not written in this book: But these are written, that ye might believe that Jesus is the Christ, the Son of God; and that believing ye might have life through his name" (John 20:30-31). John often used the word "signs" in his writings. The Greek word, *semeion*, sometimes translated "miracle," literally means something that is astonishing, very outstanding, something quite marked. Paul characterized the Jews by saying "the Jews require a sign" (1 Corinthians 1:22). The Old Testament has many references to the reality of the Hebrew people as a sign-seeking people. John saw a great sign in heaven, which was the sky above him and the sky above all of us.

What he saw was **"a woman clothed with the sun, and the moon under her feet, and upon her head a crown of twelve stars"** (12:1b). In the Old Testament the figure of a woman often refers to the church or God's people. "For thy Maker *is* thine husband; the LORD of hosts *is* his name; and thy Redeemer the Holy One of Israel; The God of the whole earth shall he be called. For the LORD hath called thee as a woman forsaken and grieved in spirit, and a wife of youth, when thou wast refused, saith thy God" (Isaiah 54:5-6). " I have likened the daughter of Zion to a comely and delicate *woman*" (Jeremiah 6:2). The New Testament also makes the same reference. "For I am jealous over you with godly jealousy: for I have espoused you to one husband, that I may present *you as* a chaste virgin to Christ" (2 Corinthians 11:2; see also Ephesians 5:25-33). So the woman here may represent the church of the Lord Jesus Christ. The woman was "clothed with the sun, and the moon under her feet, and upon her head a crown of twelve stars." The 12 stars here probably represent either the 12 patriarchs of Israel or the 12 apostles of the Lamb.

"And she being with child cried, travailing in birth, and pained to be delivered" (12:2).

While some see the woman as representative of the church in the Messianic community, the metaphor seems to shift in the next few verses where the language suggests the details surrounding Mary and the birth of Jesus. It was God's faithful people who produced Mary through the prophesied lineage.

"And there appeared another wonder in heaven; and behold a great red dragon, having seven heads and ten horns, and seven crowns upon his heads" (12:3).

The dragon in the book of Revelation is the devil himself. The red dragon would indicate a dragon of war and the seven heads either referred to seven Roman emperors between Augustus and Domitian, who reached such prominence in the Roman Empire that men built temples to worship them or it referred to the seven hills of ancient Rome. The 10 horns evidently have reference to ten kings in the provinces of the Roman Empire. The seven crowns or diadems were emblematic of royalty.

"And his tail drew the third part of the stars of heaven, and did cast them to the earth: and the dragon stood before the woman which was ready to be delivered, for to devour her child as soon as it was born" (12:4).

We read about this in the gospel of Matthew. Herod the Great attempted to destroy the newborn Jesus after the wise men, having seen his star in the East and come from afar, announced His birth. Herod attempted to get rid of Jesus by having all male children under two years of age in Bethlehem killed.

"And she brought forth a man child, who was to rule all nations with a rod of iron: and her child was caught up unto God, and *to* his throne" (12:5).

The second psalm, referring to the Messiah, speaks of the coming Lord who will rule with a rod of iron.

"And the woman fled into the wilderness, where she hath a place prepared of God, that they should feed her there a thousand two hundred *and* threescore days" (12:6).

These are 1,260 days or three and a half years. This is the time of the Jewish-Roman War, which broke out in the last part of A.D. 66 and closed in the year A.D. 70 with the destruction of Jerusalem.

"And there was war in heaven: Michael and his angels fought against the dragon; and the dragon fought and his angels, And prevailed not; neither was their place found any more in heaven. And the great dragon was cast out, that old serpent, called the Devil, and Satan, which deceiveth the whole world: he was cast out into the earth, and his angels were cast out with him. And I heard a loud voice saying in heaven, Now is come salvation, and strength, and the kingdom of our God, and the power of his Christ: for the accuser of our brethren is cast down, which accused them before our God day and night" (12:7-10).

The word "Satan" literally means "Accuser." When the sons of God were going up and down in the earth, Satan was among them. When he and God met, God asked Satan if he had tried His servant Job. Satan replied that he had not, but that Job was only serving God for what he could get out of Him (Job 1:6-12). The rest of the story is well known.

"And they overcame him by the blood of the Lamb, and by the word of their testimony; and they loved not their lives unto the death. Therefore rejoice, *ye* heavens, and ye that dwell in them. Woe to the inhabiters of the earth and of the sea! for the devil is come down unto you, having great wrath, because he knoweth that he hath but a short time. And when the dragon saw that he was cast unto the earth, he persecuted the woman which brought forth the man *child*" (12:11-13).

The casting of the dragon down from heaven to earth is symbolic of a binding of Satan, of a restraint of Satan's power in that time, because we know the devil was on earth long before this time. He appeared in the morning of time in the Garden of Eden. He existed all through the Old Testament and New Testament eras, he is existing now, and he will until the end of time. So this is a figure of speech to indicate the binding of his work and influence, a restraint of it upon earth.

"And to the woman were given two wings of a great eagle, that she might fly into the wilderness, into her place, where she is nourished for a time, and times, and half a time, from the face of the serpent" (12:14).

The book of Daniel refers to the "time, and times, and half a time." They are equivalent to three and one half years or 1260 days.

"And the serpent cast out of his mouth water as a flood after the woman, that he might cause her to be carried away of the flood. And the earth helped the woman, and the earth opened her mouth, and swallowed up the flood which the dragon cast out of his mouth. And the dragon was wroth with the woman, and went to make war with the remnant of her seed, which keep the commandments of God, and have the testimony of Jesus Christ" (12:15-17).

Revelation 12 tells us about the birth of the Lord Jesus Christ to the virgin Mary. After the birth of Jesus, the devil became exceedingly active in trying to destroy Him. When the devil and Jesus met in the great temptation in the wilderness, the destiny of the world was in the balance. The first Adam succumbed to him, but the second Adam in the wilderness of temptation was entirely successful in the encounter.

The woman fleeing into the wilderness tells us of the fleeing of the church of God when Rome destroyed Jerusalem. The Christians fled across the Jordan to ancient Pella. Abundant documentation from the early church fathers attests to this reality. The Christians fled the city to avoid destruction. While many of the Jews died, some fled to Jabneh, where the Pharisees sought to preserve Judaism.

This is an easily understood chapter, a chapter that concerns itself with the great confrontation between the church and the empire, between God and the devil, between Christ and the Caesars, between monotheism and polytheism, and between everything that was right and everything that was wrong.

CHAPTER 9

THE MARK OF THE BEAST

Revelation 13

As Revelation 13 begins, John is on the Isle of Patmos, surrounded by the Aegean Sea.

"And I stood upon the sand of the sea and I saw a beast rise up out of the sea, having seven heads and ten horns" (13:1a).

That sea from which he saw a beast arise was not the Aegean Sea, but the Tyrrhenian, which bordered the territory and the land of Italy, where the Roman Empire had its capital, where the imperial palaces stretched out along the lazy Tiber. This beast that John saw had seven heads and ten horns. The seven heads are the seven emperors from Augustus Caesar to Flavius Domitianus, emperors who reigned with such distinction that men erected Roman temples to each of them. Men worshiped them as Lord and God in these temples. This worship, however, was an evolutionary matter, and it was to the time of Domitian. There was a mandate that every occupant of the Greco-Roman world with the exception of the Jews should worship the Roman emperor as God and as Lord.

The 10 horns represent the 10 Parthian kings. Among the empires of the world surrounding the Roman world, the Parthian empire was the only one that the Romans could not conquer. The Parthians were cavalrymen. They fought upon horses. The heads of their horses were equipped for fighting their tails equipped so that they fought going and coming. After they fought with the offensive, they fought with the defensive. The Romans could not compete with this, so the Parthians naturally were the greatest danger to the Roman world.

"And upon his horns, ten crowns, and upon his heads the name of blasphemy" (13:1b).

From the beginning to the end of the book of Revelation the beast is the Roman emperor and the Roman empire. Both are synonymous in the minds of the Roman people of the Greco-Roman world.

"And the beast which I saw was like unto a leopard, and his feet were as *the feet* of a bear, and his mouth as the mouth of a lion: and the dragon gave him his power, and his seat, and great authority" (13:2). The dragon throughout the book of Revelation is the devil himself. As a result, we have introduced to us the devil himself and the Roman emperor.

"And I saw one of his heads as if it were wounded to death; and his deadly wound was healed: and all the world wondered after the beast. And they worshiped the dragon which gave power unto the beast: and they worshiped the beast, saying, Who *is* like unto the beast? who is able to make war with him? And there was given unto him a mouth speaking great things and blasphemies; and power was given unto him to continue forty *and* two months" (13:3-5). Forty and two months are three and a half years, the duration of the Jewish-Roman War.

"And he opened his mouth in blasphemy against God, to blaspheme his name, and his tabernacle, and them that dwell in heaven. And it was given unto him to make war with the saints, and to overcome them: and power was given him over all kindreds, and tongues, and nations. And all that dwell upon the earth shall worship him, whose names are not written in the book of life of the Lamb slain from the foundation of the world" (13:6-8).

All power is with God, but God across the centuries gave power to outstanding generals and leaders like Nebuchadnezzar and Cyrus, so-called great, and he used some of these men to bring the children of God to their knees as they had forsaken and were forsaking Him.

"If any man have an ear, let him hear" (13:9).

This is the admonition we teach from the seven letters to the seven churches of Asia Minor.

"He that leadeth into captivity shall go into captivity: he that killeth with the sword must be killed with the sword. Here is the patience and the faith of the saints" (13:10).

Revelation 13:1-10 concerns the Roman emperor himself. Verses 11-18 deal with the priestly caucus across the Roman world, whose authority and whose responsibility were to execute the worship of the Roman emperor.

"And I beheld another beast coming up out of the earth; and he had two horns like a lamb, and he spake as a dragon. And he exerciseth all the power of the first beast before him" (13:11-12a), that is, the emperor. In other words, he was the representative, the executor of the emperor and of his commands.

"And causeth the earth and them which dwell therein to worship the first beast, whose deadly wound was healed" (13:12b).

He was Nero Caesar who became emperor elected by the Praetorian Roman guard at the age of 17. He was wise enough for 10 years to lean upon the council of the distinguished Roman statesman, Seneca, and of the president of the Praetorian guard. But, when he became 27 years of age, he felt that he could run the Roman Empire. But his control gave way to absolute domination. In time he saw that the Roman Senate was going to condemn him to death. He fled Rome four miles out in the country to an abandoned house and took with him his most trusted servant. Nero started to commit suicide, but lacking the courage to carry through with it, he forced his attendant to complete the job. Nero died in this little house.

A rumor spread widely. Many people believed that Nero did not die but fled to Parthia and was going to gather a Parthian army and come back to the Roman world and establish his headquarters either in Antioch of Syria or upon the Tiber. Many people believed this. John had to deal with it and speak the truth concerning it. This is what is being talked about just here.

"And he doeth great wonders, so that he maketh fire come down from heaven on the earth in the sight of men" (13:13). Most men accepted this because there was the general belief of the men of the first and second centuries that this could easily happen.

"And deceiveth them that dwell on the earth by *the means of* those miracles which he had power to do in the sight of the beast; saying to them that dwell on the earth, that they should make an image to the beast, which had the wound by a sword, and did live. And he had power to give life unto the image of the beast, that the image of the beast should both speak, and cause that as

many as would not worship the image of the beast should be killed" (13:14-15).

In the worship of Flavius Domitianus, a priest might stand behind a lectern and using ventriloquism, speak as if it were Domitian speaking. Those who heard could believe it was Domitian. With Domitian speaking, they are going to bow and worship all the more. Note the last clause of verse 15, "and cause that as many as would not worship the image of the beast should be killed." It was either worship the image of the beast and live or refuse to worship him and be killed. There was no middle ground. Multiplied thousands of Christians across the Roman world gave their lives because they would not compromise the firm belief on which they had lived, which they had taught, that Almighty God and Jesus Christ are only Lord and God.

While in the Roman world, we turn to the city of Pergamum, where Satan's throne was, where men erected the imperial temple skyward, and where men and women, the hundreds who lived in Pergamum, were worshiping the Roman emperor. It's Lord's Day evening. The sun has set across the western hills of Asia Minor. Members of the church slowly make their way after dark because it is against the law to assemble for worship, making their way to a certain building. Maybe it is better to say they met in different homes. We are present on a Sunday night. We see two mothers who meet each other upstairs. One falls into the arms of another and says, "Mary, do you know what happened in our family this week?" Mary will say, "No. I'd like to know if you would like for me to know." She will say, "Well, my husband was thrown to the lions because he refused to worship Domitian as Lord and God."

A father meets another father and he says to him, "John, do you know what occurred in our household this week?" He says, "No. I'd like to know if you want me to." He says, "Our oldest son was burned at the stake because he refused to worship Domitian as Lord and God." Those things happened.

"And he causeth all, both small and great, rich and poor, free and bond, to receive a mark in their right hand, or in their foreheads: And that no man might buy or sell, save he that had the mark, or the name of the beast, or the number of his name" (13:16-17).

Picture a brother and sister living outside the city of Smyrna. It is the year 95 A.D. They are gardeners. They take what they have raised to sell into the city of Smyrna in one of the Roman markets. Our brother goes up to the manager of that market and says, "I am a farmer. My family and I have raised a large crop of vegetables and other kindred things. I would like to sell them to you and buy some groceries and some clothes for my family for the coming winter." The manager of the market looks at him and says, "Mister, have you worshiped the Roman emperor as God and as Lord? If so, do you have any evidence that you have so done?" He will say, "I have not worshiped Domitian as Lord and God because I do not believe he is. Now therefore, I have no evidence of having worshiped him." The manager will say, "I cannot buy anything from you, neither can I sell you anything." The Romans placed economic pressure on the Christians across the Roman world!

Those who worshiped the Roman emperor were required to request and receive a certificate in order to buy and sell, to go in and out of certain programs and other places in the Roman world, as if they were Roman citizens. The request read:

> To those who have been appointed to preside over the sacrifices, from Inares Akeus, from the village of Theoxonis, together with his children, Aias and Hera who reside in the village of Theadelphia. We have always sacrificed to the gods and now, in your presence and according to the regulations, we have sacrificed and offered libations, and tasted the sacred things, and we ask that you give us a certification that we have done so.

> May you fare well.

The certificate read:

> We, the representatives of the Emperor, Serenos and Hermas have seen you sacrificing.

This comes from William Barclay's second volume of his commentary on the book of Revelation.

"Here is wisdom. Let him that hath understanding count the number of the beast: for it is the number of a man" – not a church as it has been contended, the Roman Catholic Church – **"and his number *is* six hundred threescore *and* six"** (13:18) or 666.

The chart which follows explains to us very clearly and definitely the mark of the beast. Until the coming of the Arabs and their giving us their numerals, the ancient peoples counted by giving a certain numerical value to the letters of their alphabet. This was how the Christians and the Romans counted, and this chart sets forth how we can identify the mark of the beast. If we could deal directly with and bring to light more of John's identification, there would not be division concerning what the mark of the beast is.

Men have written more commentaries on the book of Revelation than on any other book in the Bible. People see so many different ideas in these commentaries that we wonder if they are talking about the same book. The problem is that they have looked at the book of Revelation, not through the eyes of the apostle John, but they have looked at it through the eyes of Charles T. Russell, the founder of Russellism, or those of Judge Rutherford (who is not a judge but Judge happened to be his first name) of New York, who lived about the 1920's, and other would-be interpreters of the book of Revelation and of the mark of the beast.

How important it is to study the book of Revelation sitting with the apostle John. If we do that we will understand what the mark of the beast is.

To follow up on what I said about the way the ancients counted, we have the Hebrew letters. The reason John used the Hebrew letters in our numerical value was because if the Roman officials saw them, they could not read Hebrew, but they could read Koine Greek. The first letter we have on the chart is the Hebrew letter *nun*, which is comparable to our N. Its numerical value is 50. The next letter is *resh*, comparable to R, and its numerical value is 200. The third letter is *vau*. Its numerical value is 6. The final *nun*, is written differently, but means the same as the nun in the main body of a Hebrew word, so we have 50 again. We add 50 to 200 to 6 to 50, which equals 306 and that spells out Nero. The reason I have a (*nun*) in parenthesis is that there are one or two inferior manuscripts, which if translated accurately would leave off this final nun. If we had time we would tell you how Irenaeus of Gaul dealt with that matter and to my thinking forever decided that the real text said only Nero.

On the next line we have the Hebrew letter *koph* which is comparable to our Q. It equals 100. We have *samech* comparable to our S. It equals 60. We have again *resh* which equals 200. So, we add these together and it comes to 360 and that equals Caesar. Adding 360 to 306 we have 666 which equals Nero Caesar. There is no question in my mind, there is no tenth of a thousandth of reservation, but that the mark of the beast was Nero Caesar, and that Nero Caesar was the mark of the beast. I think we can say that Nero Caesar was the meanest man that ever lived. Christians looked at him that way. The sane people of the Roman world so considered him. So, down the pages of Biblical history he has by the good readers and interpreters been interpreted as the mark of the beast for he was very, very beastly.

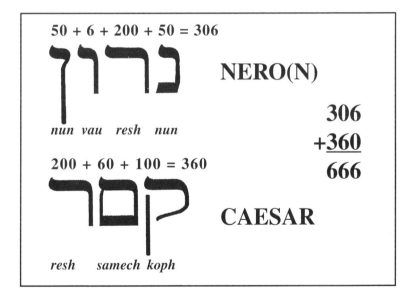

50 + 6 + 200 + 50 = 306

נרון

nun vau resh nun

200 + 60 + 100 = 360

קסר

resh samech koph

NERO(N)

306
+360
666

CAESAR

CHAPTER 10

THE TABLES ARE TURNED

Revelation 14-15

"And I looked," that is John looked, **"and, lo, a Lamb stood on the mount Sion, and with him an hundred forty** *and* **four thousand, having his Father's name written in their foreheads"** (14:1). In Revelation 13:1, John saw a beast coming up out of the sea, having 10 horns and seven heads. This beast that John saw as he looked across the Mediterranean and Aegean Seas was the beastly Roman Emperor Domitian. In complete contrast to this, he sees here in Revelation 14 the Lord Jesus Christ, the Lamb of God, standing not upon a restless sea, but upon Mount Zion (Sion). In Old Testament times and in subsequent times, Mount Zion always referred to victory. Hebrews 12:22 refers to Mount Zion as the location of the church of the living God, the immovable kingdom. "But ye are come unto mount Sion, and unto the city of the living God, the heavenly Jerusalem" (Hebrews 12:22). The word of the Lord was to go forth from Jerusalem, which is Mount Zion.

John saw 144,000. These 144,000 most probably are the same as the 144,000 of Revelation 7. This great number has the name of the Lord Jesus Christ and the name of God the Father written on their foreheads. In Revelation 7, we find the intermission between the sixth and seventh seals and the command to hold back the wind until God sealed His servants in their foreheads. In Revelation 3:12, John, in writing to the church in Philadelphia, told the Christians that they would have the name of God, the name of the city of God, and the name of the Lord Jesus Christ inscribed upon them. The name here does not mean the name of the individual but rather the ones to whom the 144,000 redeemed belonged. In ancient times, as we have pointed out, sealing indicated ownership. In the cult of Dionysius in Egypt, a certain sealing indicated the members of the cult who belonged to the god Dionysius.

"And I heard a voice from heaven, as the voice of many waters, and as the voice of a great thunder: and I heard the voice of harpers harping with their harps" (14:2).

This is a figure of speech talking about these things *as* the voice of many waters, *as* the voice of a great thunder, and *as* the voice of harpers harping with their harps. He did not actually hear harpers harping with their harps, but what he heard was *as* the *voice* of harpers harping with their harps. It would not have been possible for these to have been actual harps because in a spiritual world like heaven things are not material. There are no grounds for having harps in the church, even if they are in heaven. Babies are in heaven, but they are not in the church.

"And they sung as it were a new song before the throne, and before the four beasts, and the elders" (14:3a).

This new song was a song of the Lamb, not the song of Moses. The song of the Lamb was the song of redemption that the children of God, the 144,000, the innumerable number in Revelation 7, have learned to sing. It is a song of redemption from their past sins made possible by the blood of the Lord Jesus Christ.

"And no man could learn that song but the hundred *and* forty *and* four thousand, which were redeemed from the earth" (14:3b). The others could not learn the song because they were not spiritually attuned for the learning of it. In his letter to the church at Corinth, the apostle Paul referred to the fact that there are some spiritually minded people and there are carnally minded people. Just as the Christian is out of place in the roadhouse, the participants in the roadhouse business would be very much out of place in the church of the living God because they are attuned to a different kind of life and different activities than those pursued by the children of God. The Christian patterns his lifestyle far from the lifestyle of those who are in the roadhouses.

"These are they which were not defiled with women; for they are virgins" (14:4a).

This does not have reference to sexual immorality but rather to the beastly Roman emperor and the worship of the beastly Roman emperor. In Old Testament times, those who "went whoring" were they who participated in the worship of their neighbors. The Israelites participated in the worship of the Canaanites, the Hittites, the Jebusites, and many other "ites," who were the neighboring peoples of the children of Israel.

"These are they which follow the Lamb whithersoever he goeth. These were redeemed from among men, *being* the first-fruits unto God and to the Lamb" (14:4b).

Concerning religion, these were virgins. God purchased these 144,000 out of every tribe, from all the peoples of the world, by the precious blood of Christ.

"And in their mouth was found no guile: for they are without fault before the throne of God" (14:5).

In Revelation 21:8 we learn that the place for liars in the world beyond this one is hell itself, but these 144,000 were not liars. They therefore were entitled to go to the beautiful home of the soul, where there is no lying.

"And I saw another angel fly in the midst of heaven, having the everlasting gospel to preach unto them that dwell on the earth, and to every nation, and kindred, and tongue, and people" (14:6). The members of the Church of Jesus Christ of Latter Day Saints, more commonly called the Mormons, say that this verse is a prophecy of the time when an angel would fly over the state of New York and deposit certain tablets, which Joseph Smith, founder of Mormonism found and deciphered for publication. But the apostle John did not remotely have this in mind. He was talking about an angel, a messenger of God, who would declare the eternal tidings of the gladsome news of the gospel of Jesus Christ.

"Saying with a loud voice, Fear God, and give glory to him" (14:7a). In Ecclesiastes 12:13 we read, "Fear God, and keep his commandments." The apostle Paul, knowing the fear of the Lord, persuaded men (2 Corinthians 5:11).

"Fear God, and give glory to him, for the hour of his judgment is come" (14:7b).

Here is a turning point in the book of Revelation. Prior to Revelation 14:7 was the hour of the Roman Empire, and Rome was punishing the children of God. The tables have now turned. The punishment turns to Rome herself, for the hour of the judgment of God is come. As Paul often quoted from the Old Testament, vengeance belongs to the Lord. "Dearly beloved, avenge not yourselves, but *rather* give place unto wrath: for it is written, Vengeance *is* mine; I will repay, saith the Lord" (Romans 12:19).

"And worship him that made heaven, and earth, and the sea, and the fountains of waters" (14:7c).

Do not worship the Roman emperor, but worship Almighty God Who is the creator of all things.

"And there followed another angel, saying, Babylon is fallen, is fallen, that great city, because she made all nations drink of the wine of the wrath of her fornication" (14:8).

This is Revelation's first announcement of the approaching fall of Rome. It is reminiscent of Isaiah 31:27 and the prophecies of Jeremiah which announce the imminent fall of Babylon on the Euphrates, the very wicked Babylon. Daniel 4:30 refers to Babylon as "the great Babylon." Here the apostle John hears the angel announcing the fall of Rome. In early Christian literature, Rome identifies with Babylon, and Babylon identifies with Rome. The Sibylline Oracles spell this out unmistakably. In 1 Peter 5:13, the apostle Peter states, "The *church that is* at Babylon, elected together with *you,* saluteth you." The church was sending greetings from New Testament Babylon, which is Rome, to those in Pontus, Galatia, Cappadocia, Bithynia, and other parts of that area (1 Peter 1:1).

"And the third angel followed them, saying with a loud voice, If any man worship the beast and his image, and receive *his* mark in his forehead, or in his hand, The same shall drink of the wine of the wrath of God, which is poured out without mixture into the cup of his indignation; and he shall be tormented with fire and brimstone in the presence of the holy angels, and in the presence of the Lamb" (14:9-10).

In chapter 13, unless you had the mark of the beast, unless you worshiped the beast, you could not buy or sell. Unless you worshiped the beast, you were subject to persecution, imprisonment and often death. Now the tables are turned, and they who have worshiped the beast, who have his image, who have received the mark on their foreheads and on their hands shall drink of the wine of the wrath of

God and "shall be tormented with fire and brimstone in the presence of the holy angels, and in the presence of the Lamb." We see how completely reversed is the situation as mirrored here in the great book of Revelation.

Rome had her day. That day was shortly to come to an end. Rome would be no more. She would fall, as great as many considered her to be, and great would be the fall thereof. But the church of the living God will not fall. She will continue to march on triumphantly. The punishment of fire and brimstone is going to be in the presence of the holy angels and in the presence of the Lamb, making it all the more terrifying and the suffering all the greater. To be burned, to be persecuted, to be killed in the presence of the righteous make it much worse. A child dislikes being punished anytime but especially so in the presence of his or her friends or in the presence of the parents' friends. The punishment here is all the greater because it is in the presence of the holy angels and Jesus.

"And the smoke of their torment ascendeth up for ever and ever: and they have no rest day nor night, who worship the beast and his image, and whosoever receiveth the mark of his name" (14:11). Now the picture is altogether different from what it has been in earlier chapters of the Revelation. **"Here is the patience of the saints: here** *are* **they that keep the commandments of God, and the faith of Jesus"** (14:12).

"And I heard a voice from heaven saying unto me, Write, Blessed *are* **the dead which die in the Lord from henceforth: Yea, saith the Spirit, that they may rest from their labours; and their works do follow them"** (14:13).

The book of Revelation has seven distinct beatitudes. Matthew records eight beatitudes from Jesus. This beatitude in Revelation 14:13 is the second of the seven. Preachers have read it more than a thousand times, perhaps more than a hundred thousand times, at funerals. The message of it is, "Blessed *are* the dead which die in the Lord." You will recall that Paul wrote to the Thessalonian Christians who had lost loved ones, "Sorrow not, even as others which have no hope" (1 Thessalonians 4:13). You have hope, but those who are not Christians do not. The blessed are those who die in the Lord not those who die out of the Lord.

"From henceforth: Yea, saith the Spirit, that they may rest from their labours; and their works do follow them" (14:13b).

That is, their works follow them after they have died, and the works follow them until the judgment day. On the world's last day, when the uncounted trillions of all times assemble before Judge Jesus, He will open the book, and He will judge the people, every man according to his works.

"And I looked, and behold a white cloud, and upon the cloud *one* **sat like unto the Son of man, having on his head a golden crown, and in his hand a sharp sickle. And another angel came out of the temple, crying with a loud voice to him that sat on the cloud, Thrust in thy sickle, and reap: for the time is come for thee to reap; for the harvest of the earth is ripe. And he that sat on the cloud thrust in his sickle on the earth; and the earth was reaped"** (14:14-16).

Verses 14 to 16 here definitely refer to a punishment visited upon the Roman people, the non-Christian Roman people.

"And another angel came out of the temple which is in heaven, he also having a sharp sickle. And another angel came out from the altar, which had power over fire; and cried with a loud cry to him that had the sharp sickle, saying, Thrust in thy sharp sickle, and gather the clusters of the vine of the earth; for her grapes are fully ripe. And the angel thrust in his sickle into the earth, and gathered the vine of the earth, and cast *it* **into the great winepress of the wrath of God"** (14:17-19).

There are some who remember making molasses. After the farmers cut the cane, the donkeys or mules would go around the circle pressing down the sugar cane. By the continuing pressing and grinding, they pressed out the molasses. This is a similar picture of what would happen to the Roman people as God pressured, pressed and punished them.

"And the winepress was trodden without the city, and blood came out of the winepress, even unto the horse bridles, by the space of a thousand *and* **six hundred furlongs"** (14:20).

This probably has reference to the destruction of Jerusalem and could have some further reference to the destruction of Rome in the fourth century of the Christian era.

Turning back to the first part of Revelation 14, let us review briefly.

The first five verses present to us a redeemed number (not a literal, but a figurative number), whom God has sealed with the seal of the living God and with the name of God and the name of Jesus, and the name of the house of God stamped upon them. They are the ones God will save. Verses 6 and 7 tell of the everlasting gospel to be proclaimed throughout the entire world. Beginning with verse 8, we have a change where the visitation of punishment is going to be upon the Roman people, not upon the children of God.

"And I saw another sign in heaven, great and marvellous, seven angels having the seven last plagues; for in them is filled up the wrath of God. And I saw as it were a sea of glass mingled with fire: and them that had gotten the victory over the beast, and over his image, and over his mark, *and* over the number of his name, stand on the sea of glass, having the harps of God. And they sing the song of Moses the servant of God, and the song of the Lamb, saying, Great and marvellous *are* thy works, Lord God Almighty; just and true *are* thy ways, thou King of saints. Who shall not fear thee, O Lord, and glorify thy name? for *thou* only *art* holy: for all nations shall come and worship before thee; for thy judgments are made manifest" (15:1-4).

Verses 3 and 4 offer up one of the great doxologies in Revelation. "Doxology" means a word of praise. It is the combination of two Greek words: *doxo*, meaning "glory, or praise," and *logos*, meaning "a word of praise, an anthem of praise."

"And after that I looked, and, behold, the temple of the tabernacle of the testimony in heaven was opened" (15:5).

This temple of the tabernacle of testimony was an assurance to the people of God that God was with them. Had not Jesus said on the mountain in Galilee to His 11 disciples, "Lo, I am with you alway, *even* unto the end of the world" (Matthew 28:20). What He said to them, He said to an innumerable number of children of God across the continents and through the centuries.

"And the seven angels came out of the temple, having the seven plagues, clothed in pure and white linen, and having their breasts girded with golden girdles. And one of the four beasts gave unto the seven angels seven golden vials full of the wrath of God, who liveth for ever and ever. And the temple was filled with smoke from the glory of God, and from his power; and no

man was able to enter into the temple, till the seven plagues of the seven angels were fulfilled" (15:6-8).

Chapter 15 is a continuation of chapter14. We have mirrored unto us this anthem of praise and glory of the greatness of God and the Lord Jesus Christ. As the Christians in ancient Smyrna sat and listened to this reading of the book of Revelation, the doxology was meaningful and encouraging. They renewed their determination to be true to God and to refuse every attempt to compromise their loyalty to the Lord Jesus Christ by worshiping the image of the Roman emperor.

CHAPTER II

THE BATTLE OF ARMAGEDDON

Revelation 16

"And I heard a great voice out of the temple saying to the seven angels, Go your ways, and pour out the vials of the wrath of God upon the earth. And the first went, and poured out his vial upon the earth; and there fell a noisome and grievous sore upon the men which had the mark of the beast, and *upon* them which worshiped his image" (16:1-2).

Again, attention returns to chapter 13. You had to have the mark of the beast to buy or sell. If you didn't have that mark you could neither buy nor sell nor live. It was determined that the authorities would kill you. But here the tables are turned. It is a different story.

"And the second angel poured out his vial upon the sea; and it became as the blood of a dead *man;* and every living soul died in the sea" (16:3).

This is reminiscent of one of the plagues that God visited upon the Egyptians when they incarcerated the Hebrews in their land.

"And the third angel poured out his vial upon the rivers and fountains of waters; and they became blood. And I heard the angel of the waters say, Thou art righteous, O Lord, which art, and wast, and shalt be, because thou hast judged thus. For they have shed the blood of saints and prophets, and thou hast given them blood to drink; for they are worthy. And I heard another out of the altar say, Even so, Lord God Almighty, true and righteous *are* thy judgments" (16:4-7).

With our imagination, we transport ourselves back to the time and places occupied by these Christians to see their reactions as they listened to this great message from heaven. The people with whom they were associated and for whom they worked told them just the contrary every day by. They told them that Rome was eternal, that the church of the Nazarene would soon be gone. They told them, when everything else passed from time, Rome would be eternal. But here a different voice, a voice from heaven, brings a different message, a message of the eternity of God. It is a message of the transitoriness of Rome and of the reality that Rome of Babylon, no matter how great men considered her to be, was going to fall.

"And the fourth angel poured out his vial upon the sun; and power was given unto him to scorch men with fire. And men were scorched with great heat, and blasphemed the name of God, which hath power over these plagues: and they repented not to give him glory. And the fifth angel poured out his vial upon the seat of the beast; and his kingdom was full of darkness; and they gnawed their tongues for pain, And blasphemed the God of heaven because of their pains and their sores, and repented not of their deeds" (16:8-11).

All of this suggests that God always has the last word. Men propose, but God disposes. The Chinese have a saying that no bird ever flies so far but his tail follows him. Far greater than the Chinese poet, Moses, speaking to the children of Israel after 40 years of trying experiences with them, stated in Numbers 32:23, "Be sure your sin will find you out." Paul said, "Be not deceived; God is not mocked: for whatsoever a man soweth, that shall he also reap. For he that soweth to his flesh shall of the flesh reap corruption; but he that soweth to the Spirit shall of the Spirit reap life everlasting" (Galatians 6:7-8). What a man sows he will reap; what a nation sows it will reap; what a people sow they will reap. So it was true in the history of ancient Rome.

The Psalmist said that all the nations that have forgotten God have gone down into the dust of the earth. Of the 19 civilizations that have marched across the pages of history, according to Arnold Toynbee, 16 of them have perished. Their perishing began inside the nation. That's where it began with Rome. She was rotten with a cancer. In Romans 1, we have a delineation of the character of the Roman people. The worst of Hollywood would appear as saints in contrast to the sins of the people of Rome. God says these sins will be reaped, and for these sins the Roman people will pay. They will not escape. **"And the sixth angel poured out his vial upon the great river Euphrates; and the water thereof was dried up, that the way of the kings of the east might be prepared"** (16:12). The river Euphrates was the eastern boundary of the Roman Empire and the western boundary for the Parthian Empire. Rome was never able to subjugate the Parthians. After the bowl was poured out on the river Euphrates, "the water thereof was dried up, that the way of the kings of the east might be prepared." The east or "sunrising" (ASV) was from Parthia.

"And I saw three unclean spirits like frogs *come* **out of the mouth of the dragon, and out of the mouth of the beast, and out of the mouth of the false prophet. For they are the spirits of devils, working miracles,** *which* **go forth unto the kings of the earth and of the whole world, to gather them to the battle of that great day of God Almighty"** (16:13-14). The third beatitude comes next: **"Behold, I come as a thief. Blessed** *is* **he that watcheth, and keepeth his garments, lest he walk naked, and they see his shame. And he gathered them together into a place called in the Hebrew tongue Armageddon"** (16:15-16).

For centuries men and women have been interested in the battle of Har-Mageddon (ASV) or Armageddon. Men have heard multiplied thousands of sermons about it and more thousands of lessons have been taught in classes. There are conscientious persons who have spent sleepless nights tossing from one side of the bed to the other, wondering if the battle of Armageddon would break out any minute. Multiplied denominations have built doctrines around the battle of Armageddon.

What did the battle of Armageddon mean to the first readers of the book of Revelation? What did it mean to the apostle John? Whatever it meant to them is what the battle of Armageddon was or is or shall be.

Armageddon was a battlefield. This battlefield began on the northwest side of Palestine at Mount Carmel. It extended across Palestine to Mount Gilboa on the southeast. Between these two mountains was a perfect plain for battles. On the plains of Megiddo, men fought hundreds of decisive battles. There were battles between the powers on the northeast and those on the southwest, between the Egyptians and the Assyrians, the Egyptians and the Babylonians, and the Egyptians and the Medes and Persians. On one occasion, Pharaoh Necho, making his way to fight the Assyrians, was intercepted by Josiah, the good king of Judah. The king of Egypt tried to dissuade him from the battle, but Josiah couldn't be persuaded and died in his chariot (2 Chronicles 35:20-24).

Barak and Deborah, with the stars fighting on their side, defeated Sisera and the Canaanites, according to Judges 5:19-20, "by the waters of Megiddo." On the plains of Megiddo, Saul and Jonathan fought their last battle with the Philistines. There the people of God defeated Antiochus Epiphanes IV, according to Daniel 11. The best blood of Israel and the worst blood of Israel's enemies soaked Armageddon. Armageddon has been the chosen place of encounter in every contest carried on in Palestine from the days of Nebuchadnezzar, king of Babylon, to the disastrous march of Napoleon Bonaparte to Syria.

The battle of Armageddon in Revelation is not a physical battle fought upon the physical plains of war with instruments of destruction, aggression and suppression, but it is a battle fought upon the battlefields of the human heart. It is a spiritual battle, a moral battle.

The first battle of Armageddon was fought in the Garden of Eden. God placed Adam and Eve in the beautiful garden, a lovely home. Through this garden ran four rivers. It had all kinds of fruit they could eat, except the fruit of the tree of knowledge of good and evil. If any people should have been happy in an environment, it was they. But into their home came the devil, the old serpent, who tempted them. We will not go into the details of the temptation, but Adam and Eve fought the battle of Armageddon and lost it. In losing the battle of Armageddon, men and women started across the stages of life beneath their burdens of sin. They offered sacrifices upon Israel's altars and Zion's hills until the man from Calvary washed their sins away.

Another encounter with the battle of Armageddon was by Joseph in the land of Egypt as a steward in Potiphar's house. Potiphar knew nothing except the fact of his own food he ate and his own personal concern, but Potiphar's wife tried to tempt Joseph to commit adultery with her. She made a number of attempts, all of which were unsuccessful. Joseph fought the battle of Armageddon and won it!

Another encounter was when David was upon the roof of his house. The houses in those days had flat roofs. His army was out in the fields of war fighting for him. As the cool of the evening came, David was walking slowly upon his house and saw a woman bathing in a nearby pool. He lusted for her and sent for her. Then he added adultery to other sins, climaxing it all in murder itself. David fought the battle of Armageddon, but he lost it.

Our Lord, after John the Baptist baptized Him in the River Jordan, was driven by the Spirit into the wilderness where He fasted for forty days and forty nights. After this, He fought the battle of Armageddon with the devil in three encounters. In the first encounter, the devil came to Him and said, "If you are the Son of God as God declared forty days ago, as it was announced from heaven, command that these stones lying out here become bread." The stones lying before Jesus looked like loaves of bread as made in the Middle East during the first century of our era.

If ever anyone was hungry, our Lord was. If ever anyone was tempted to turn stones into bread, it must have been our Lord, for He was tempted in all points like as we are, yet He was without sin. But He replied to the devil, with whom He was fighting the battle of Armageddon, "It is written, That man shall not live by bread alone, but by every word of God" (Luke 4:4), quoting the book of Deuteronomy.

Then the devil took Him unto an exceedingly high mountain. He showed Him all the kingdoms of the world in their resplendent glory. He could see the Nile as it ran like a blue ribbon out to the sea. He could see the Tiber as it lazily made its way through the city of Rome. He could see the imperial palace of the reigning emperor. He could see Ephesus in all its wealth and glory, Antioch, Assyria, Corinth and Alexandria, all the kingdoms of the world and their glory. Satan offered them all to our Lord if he would merely fall down and worship him. But He said to the devil, "Get thee behind me, Satan: for it is written, Thou shalt worship the Lord thy God, and him only shalt thou serve" (Luke 4:8). The first commandment stated: "I am the

LORD thy God, which have brought thee out of the land of Egypt, out of the house of bondage. Thou shalt have no other gods before me" (Exodus 20:2-3).

Then the devil took Jesus up into the holy city. He set Him on the pinnacle of the temple and said, "If what God said forty days ago is true, cast yourself down from this pinnacle into the valley, for it is written: He shall give his angels charge over thee, to keep thee: and in their hands they shall bear thee up, lest at any time thou dash thy foot against a stone" (Luke 4:10-11). The devil cited Scripture, but he did not cite it accurately. In Eden he added to it, and in the wilderness temptation he took from it, for the psalm from which he quoted, when stated in its fullness, says that God will take care of those who trust in Him. Jesus would not have trusted in Him if He had jumped from the pinnacle. He would have trusted in the devil.

There was a common belief among the apocalyptists of Judaism that he who was able to jump from the pinnacle of the temple unharmed would be the Messiah for whom the Jews had long been looking. This added to the temptation. That Jesus was in the holy precincts of the temple also added to it, but as He encountered the devil "face to face" he said, "It is said, Thou shalt not tempt the Lord thy God" (Luke 4:12). He won the battle of Armageddon.

Our Lord met the devil in three encounters in the battle of Armageddon in the wilderness after John baptized him in the Jordan. He came triumphantly out of all three encounters, victorious over the devil. He triumphantly won the battle of Armageddon.

In Romans 7 Paul wrote to the Roman church and to us, "When I would do good, evil is present with me" (Romans 7:21). He said there's always a war in my members, a battle between evil and good. What Paul stated to the Roman Christians and to the Christians of all times has been and will ever be true of the experiences of men and women, particularly the children of God. You and I are fighting the battle of Armageddon every day and every night. We are having to make a choice between right and wrong. After Joshua had led the children of Israel, he said to them in his farewell address, "Choose you this day whom ye will serve" (Joshua 24:15). Our Lord said, "No man can serve two masters: for either he will hate the one, and love the other; or else he will hold to the one, and despise the other. Ye cannot serve God and mammon" (Matthew 6:24). Then in

Matthew 12:30 He said, "He that is not with me is against me; and he that gathereth not with me scattereth abroad."

The battle of Armageddon, I repeat, is not a battle pitched upon the physical fields of carnal warfare, but it is a battle that you and I fight every day. Some fight it every hour of every day, a battle between right and wrong. It is a battle, in a sense, between the church and the world, between the devil and God, between the Caesars and Christ, between the church and the Roman Empire, and between monotheism and polytheism. It is a great battle, far greater and more significant than battles fought with carnal weapons.

The church will be triumphant! We read in Daniel 2:44, "In the days of these kings shall the God of heaven set up a kingdom, which shall never be destroyed: and the kingdom shall not be left to other people, *but* it shall break in pieces and consume all these kingdoms, and it shall stand for ever." "The gates of Hades shall not prevail against it" (Matthew 16:18), the onward march of the church of the living God. In the battle of Armageddon, victory always belongs to the church and the people of God who are the church.

The chapter concludes with further descriptions of the power of God over Rome. **"And the seventh angel poured out his vial into the air; and there came a great voice out of the temple of heaven, from the throne, saying, It is done. And there were voices, and thunders, and lightnings; and there was a great earthquake, such as was not since men were upon the earth, so mighty an earthquake, *and* so great. And the great city was divided into three parts, and the cities of the nations fell: and great Babylon came in remembrance before God, to give unto her the cup of the wine of the fierceness of his wrath. And every island fled away, and the mountains were not found. And there fell upon men a great hail out of heaven, *every stone* about the weight of a talent: and men blasphemed God because of the plague of the hail; for the plague thereof was exceeding great"** (16:17-21).

CHAPTER 12

JUDGMENT OF THE GREAT WHORE

Revelation 17

"And there came one of the seven angels which had the seven vials, and talked with me, saying unto me, Come hither; I will show unto thee the judgment of the great whore that sitteth upon many waters" (17:1).

These seven angels are the seven angels of presence, as discussed earlier. The book of Tobit names these seven angels, although Scripture only names Gabriel and Michael. One of these seven angels came to the apostle John and said, "I will show unto thee the judgment of the great whore that sitteth upon many waters." The word "judgment" is a translation of the Greek word *krima*, which the Greek Septuagint Old Testament uses to refer to the ancient city of Babylon upon the Euphrates. To the first century Christians, "harlot" always referred to Rome, since it always referred to an enemy, such as Babylon, Tyre or Nineveh. Nahum spoke of Nineveh. Jeremiah and Isaiah spoke of Babylon. The Babylon of the Old Testament was the Rome of the New Testament, and the Rome of the New Testament was the Babylon of the Old Testament. Peter said, "The *church that is* at Babylon, elected together with *you,* saluteth you" (1 Peter 5:13), or "she that is in Rome salutes you."

In the *Sibylline Oracles* we have Rome identified with Babylon and Babylon identified with Rome. So the counterpart of Old Testament Babylon was New Testament Rome. She "that sitteth upon many waters" refers to the prominent location of the Roman Empire, around which were the Mediterranean, the Black, the

Caspian, the Aegean and other seas.

"With whom the kings of the earth have committed fornication, and the inhabitants of the earth have been made drunk with the wine of her fornication" (17:2).

This, of course, is a figure of speech that refers to illicit connections with the Roman Empire – illicit connections of drunkenness, idolatry and illicit relations.

"So he carried me away in the spirit into the wilderness: and I saw a woman sit upon a scarlet coloured beast, full of names of blasphemy, having seven heads and ten horns" (17:3).

A scarlet colored beast would indicate great wickedness. Not only was the beast scarlet colored, but it also was the Roman emperor, and this Roman emperor or beast had names full of blasphemy. These names were the names they called themselves: "Lord and God." Domitian, during whose reign John wrote the book of Revelation, issued his decrees as "Lord God Domitianus" and such. So it was unmistakable in the minds of those who heard this book read that John referred to Domitian. He had seven heads and ten horns. The seven heads referred to the seven hills of ancient Rome. Every October there was a commemoration to the fact that seven hills enclosed Rome.

"And the woman was arrayed in purple and scarlet colour, and decked with gold and precious stones and pearls, having a golden cup in her hand full of abominations and filthiness of her fornication: And upon her forehead *was* **a name written, MYSTERY, BABYLON THE GREAT, THE MOTHER OF HARLOTS AND ABOMINATIONS OF THE EARTH"** (17:4-5).

Daniel 4 calls Babylon the great, but here John refers without mistake to ancient Rome, not to papal Rome, but to ancient Rome.

"And I saw the woman drunken with the blood of the saints, and with the blood of the martyrs of Jesus: and when I saw her, I wondered with great admiration. And the angel said unto me, Wherefore didst thou marvel? I will tell thee the mystery of the woman, and of the beast that carrieth her, which hath the seven heads and ten horns. The beast that thou sawest was, and is not; and shall ascend out of the bottomless pit, and go into perdition: and they that dwell on the earth shall wonder, whose names were not written in the book of life from the foundation of the

world, when they behold the beast that was, and is not, and yet is" (17:6-8).

This beast is identified with Nero. Many doubted that Nero committed suicide in a house four miles outside Rome but believed that he fled to Parthia and was going to gather a Parthian army, return to Rome, unseat the emperor upon the Tiber and again rule over the Roman Empire. The last one to claim to be this Roman emperor was Domitian, who made the claim in his early years. He began to reign in A.D. 81 and closed his reign in A.D. 96, when enemies killed him. Since there was no pretender for the Neronian place, some believed that he was going to come up from the abyss.

"And here *is* the mind which hath wisdom. The seven heads are seven mountains, on which the woman sitteth. And there are seven kings" (17:9-10a).

As we have explained, the seven mountains are the hills of Rome.

"Five are fallen, and one is, *and* the other is not yet come; and when he cometh, he must continue a short space" (19:10b).

The king that "is" was in all probability Vespasian. The one who would continue only a "short space" must have been his son Titus, who reigned only two years.

"And the beast that was, and is not, even he is the eighth, and is of the seven, and goeth into perdition. And the ten horns which thou sawest are ten kings, which have received no kingdom as yet; but receive power as kings one hour with the beast" (17:11-12).

These were men who aspired to be kings in the provinces of the Roman Empire.

"These have one mind, and shall give their power and strength unto the beast. These shall make war with the Lamb, and the Lamb shall overcome them: for he is Lord of lords, and King of kings: and they that are with him *are* called, and chosen, and faithful" (17:13-14).

We find expressed here the theme of the entire book of Revelation, that He is Lord of lords and King of kings. The Christians heard on every hand, as we've said a number of times, that the Roman emperor was Lord of lords and King of kings. The Roman Empire was eternal. All roads led to Rome, and all roads led out of Rome. Here is a message from heaven that says this is not true. The reality of the matter is that Jesus Christ is Lord of lords, and He is King of kings.

"And he saith unto me, The waters which thou sawest, where the whore sitteth, are peoples, and multitudes, and nations, and tongues" (17:15).

We've already stated that water surrounded the Roman Empire on every frontier.

"And the ten horns which thou sawest upon the beast, these shall hate the whore, and shall make her desolate and naked, and shall eat her flesh, and burn her with fire" (17:16).

This probably has reference to civil war in which they turn against the Roman emperor.

"For God hath put in their hearts to fulfill his will, and to agree, and give their kingdom unto the beast, until the words of God shall be fulfilled. And the woman which thou sawest is" the Roman Catholic Church. I put that incorrectly on purpose because so many have believed that the woman was papal Rome, the Roman Catholic Church. Martin Luther held this view. So far as I know, it started with him. It was natural for him to hold that view. As one generation handed down this view to the next generation, various ones accepted it, even Alexander Campbell. But here John, whom I follow, said that **"the woman which thou sawest is that great city, which reigneth over the kings of the earth"** (17:17-18). What city? The city of Rome. Now isn't that plain? That's just as plain as Acts 2:38, "Then Peter said unto them, Repent, and be baptized every one of you in the name of Jesus Christ for the remission of sins, and ye shall receive the gift of the Holy Ghost." This great city, not the Roman Catholic Church, reigns over the kings of the earth. That is what she was doing in the first century of our era, shortly before that time, and certainly for about 300 years afterward.

Chapter 17 is a spelling out in detail of what Revelation 14:8 announced, "Babylon is fallen, is fallen, that great city." Then in Revelation 16:19: "And the great city was divided into three parts, and the cities of the nations fell: and great Babylon came in remembrance before God, to give unto her the cup of the wine of the fierceness of his wrath." Remember Revelation 14:7, the turning point of the book: "Fear God, and give glory to him; for the hour of his judgment is come: and worship him that made heaven, and earth, and the sea, and the fountains of waters." The hour of the judgment of God is come. The tables are turned. Things are reversed. God has always been in the saddle, but He's going to exercise His authority. The church of God will march victoriously on while Rome, decadent inside with cancer, is going to fall. Just as sure as Rome was, Rome will not be. In the year 476, in the hands of the barbarians from the North, Rome with all that was Rome would fall. That is what Revelation 17 and Revelation 18 are unmistakably describing. What a great consolation, what a tremendous encouragement that was to the children of God, tossed to and fro, persecuted by the Romans. They had lost members of their families who were fed to the lions in the coliseum, who were burned at the stake to illuminate Roman skies at night, who were hunted by a pack of savage hounds as their tormentors dressed Christians in the skins of wild animals. Those were times that tried the souls of men. How great it was that they could hear a message from heaven, that they could know the realities of what was going on, that God was still in control, that it would not be long before Rome would be no more and the church would march on and on. In the year 325 Constantine pronounced the Christian religion and the church of the Lord Jesus Christ as the official religion of the Roman Empire. The gates of Hades will not prevail against it. It is an immovable kingdom which stall stand forever.

Chapter 18 continues the message of chapter 17. It demonstrates in no uncertain terms, "Fallen, fallen is Babylon the great." The merchants of the earth from near and far moan and bemoan that their merchandise will no longer continue and that the great mercantile commercial city of Rome will fall.

CHAPTER 13

THE FALL OF BABYLON

Revelation 18

Revelation 18 begins with **"after these things"** (v. 1a). The things John has in mind are the things in chapters 16 and 17. John **"saw another angel come down from heaven,"** an angel other than the one that came down and who narrated to John the meaning of the vision of chapter 17. This angel coming down from heaven, **"having great power,"** had great authority. This authority came from heaven. Jesus had said that "all power [or authority] is given unto me in heaven and in earth" (Matthew 28:18).

"And the earth was lightened with his glory" (18:1b).

The book of Isaiah refers to the heavens being lightened with the glory of God. Luke 2 refers to the angels of glory who joined in a doxology to the shepherds watching flocks at night on the Judean hills. Luke says that the glory of God surrounded those angels.

"And he [the angel] **cried mightily with a strong voice, saying, Babylon the great is fallen, is fallen, and is become the habitation of devils, and the hold of every foul spirit, and a cage of every unclean and hateful bird"** (18:2).

This statement reminds us of similar statements made by Daniel and Jeremiah concerning the fall of Old Testament Babylon. Babylon was a fabulous city with a high wall that went around it and six chariots could go abreast at the same time. We talk about interstate highways, speedways and such, but we don't have anything that surpasses what they had in Babylon, at least as far as room. This ancient city sat on the Euphrates River. The river ran through the city.

The city had elaborate and beautiful gardens; it was one of the wonders of the world in its day. Everyone looked upon it with great reverence and awe as a city that was tremendous. Daniel called it the "great Babylon." Everywhere anyone spoke of Babylon it was the great Babylon. But this Babylon, as great as she was, seated upon the Euphrates River, was going to fall according to Isaiah and Jeremiah. She did fall. Great was her fall. So great was it that she was completely uninhabited. Replacing human beings in inhabiting the city were demons. The city was a stronghold for every unclean spirit and a cage for every unclean and hateful bird.

We have learned that the Babylon of the Old Testament is the Rome of the New Testament. Peter, writing to the churches of Bithynia and adjacent provinces, said, "The *church that is* at Babylon, elected together with *you,* saluteth you" (1 Peter 5:13), that is, the church in Rome salutes you. The *Sybilline Oracles* and other noncanonical literature of New Testament times and the early days of the church, identify Old Testament Babylon and New Testament Rome as one and the same.

"For all nations have drunk of the wine of the wrath of her fornication, and the kings of the earth have committed fornication with her, and the merchants of the earth are waxed rich through the abundance of her delicacies" (18:3).

The fornication of Rome is not necessarily illicit relations, but by way of figure of speech, it refers to her relations with the nations of the world. Because of their involvement with Rome, they will suffer with her in her fall. They will fall along with Rome.

"And I heard another voice from heaven, saying, Come out of her, my people, that ye be not partakers of her sins, and that ye receive not of her plagues. For her sins have reached unto heaven, and God hath remembered her iniquities" (18:4-5).

Isaiah and Jeremiah urged the people to come forth from ancient Tyre and Babylon. The application here is to the people of God to come forth out of New Testament Rome and not to receive her plagues, "for her sins have reached unto heaven, and God hath remembered her iniquities." Her sins were so great that they had reached beyond earth and had gone skyward, even unto heaven itself, and God had remembered the iniquities of ancient Babylon and of New Testament Rome. Romans 1:18-32 describes the wickedness of the Roman world. It was a very immoral world, a very wicked world. The Holy Spirit spared no words as he guided Paul in describing the awfulness and the sinfulness of the Roman world.

"Reward her even as she rewarded you, and double unto her double according to her works: in the cup which she hath filled fill to her double. How much she hath glorified herself, and lived deliciously, so much torment and sorrow give her: for she saith in her heart, I sit a queen, and am no widow, and shall see no sorrow" (18:6-7).

Revelation 14:7 was the turning point of the book. The Holy Spirit stated, "Fear God, and give glory to him; for the hour of his judgment is come." The hour of judgment is come to Rome. The tables had turned. Not the people of God, but the people of Rome will be punished. You know that in the affairs of God, He always has the last word. He has the last say in everything. Paul said, "Be not deceived; God is not mocked: for whatsoever a man soweth, that shall he also reap. For he that soweth to his flesh shall of the flesh reap corruption; but he that soweth to the Spirit shall of the Spirit reap life everlasting" (Galatians 6:7-8). With forty years of experience leading the children of Israel, Moses said to them, "be sure your sin will find you out" (Numbers 32:23). There is no truth more true than that. Wherever men have sinned, their sins have found them out. We cannot get away from the sins we commit. They will follow us.

Here is what the Lord is saying about Rome. In Exodus 20:5-6 the Lord said to Moses, "I the LORD thy God *am* a jealous God, visiting the iniquity of the fathers upon the children unto the third and fourth *generation* of them that hate me; And showing mercy unto thousands of them that love me, and keep my commandments." The very bad thing about Rome was that she felt her pride, **"for she saith in her heart, I sit a queen, and am no widow, and shall see no sorrow"** (18:7b).

"Therefore shall her plagues come in one day, death, and mourning, and famine; and she shall be utterly burned with fire: for strong *is* the Lord God who judgeth her" (18:8).

Solomon said, "Pride *goeth* before destruction, and an haughty spirit before a fall" (Proverbs 16:18). The pages of history abundantly testify to the truth of this. One of the most serious things wrong with the church in Laodicea, as revealed in chapter three, was that she did not realize her lukewarmness. She was not aware of the fact that she needed anything. In fact, she said, "I don't need anything. I have everything." Whenever a person reaches that state, he is in a miserably poor condition. We must always feel as Isaiah wrote, that "we are all as an unclean *thing,* and all our righteousnesses *are* as filthy rags" (Isaiah 64:6) in God's sight. But Rome was not remotely conscious of this reality of her condition.

"And the kings of the earth, who have committed fornication and lived deliciously with her, shall bewail her, and lament for her, when they shall see the smoke of her burning, Standing afar off for the fear of her torment, saying, Alas, alas, that great city Babylon, that mighty city! for in one hour is thy judgment come" (18:9-10).

According to legend, Romulus and Remus built Rome some 800 years before. Of course, centuries passed after the first century, because Rome did not fall until A.D. 476. But she fell. According to the length of her history, the time in which she fell was comparable to one hour.

Nations have risen across centuries but have fallen in decades. Churches have risen across scores of years and grown across these years but have markedly declined within a decade. Upon their wall could be written "Ichabod" (1 Samuel 4:21). They're dead. They're gone. There are men in the church who have risen to great eminence, whose names have been household names across our great brotherhood, in whose names countless people have put utmost confidence. Yet we have known all the confidence they built up, all the good that they did, to be gone, relatively speaking, in an hour's time. Nothing is more true than the truth that our sins will find us out.

"And the merchants of the earth shall weep and mourn over her; for no man buyeth their merchandise any more: The merchandise of gold, and silver, and precious stones, and of pearls, and fine linen, and purple, and silk, and scarlet, and all thyine wood, and all manner vessels of ivory, and all manner of vessels of most precious wood, and of brass, and iron, and marble, And cinnamon, and odours, and ointments, and frankincense, and wine, and oil, and fine flour, and wheat, and beasts, and sheep, and horses, and chariots, and slaves, and souls of men" (18:11-13).

Rome was a great commercial empire, one of the largest commercial trading empires the world has ever known. Traders from the Far East, from China and India, made their way upon camels laden with ivory and silk and the finest merchandise that came from the East. Merchandise came from the West by way of Rome and Corinth and Ephesus, from the North by way of Antioch of Syria, and from the South by way of Alexandria of Egypt. The traders met in the commercial marts of the Roman Empire. All of this commerce would cease at the fall of Rome. Rome would fall because her sins had reached high into heaven. The chief sin was the persecution of the children of God by feeding them to the lions in the coliseum and in the arenas of the Roman Empire and by burning them at the stake in a thousand places.

"And the fruits that thy soul lusted after are departed from thee, and all things which were dainty and goodly are departed from thee, and thou shalt find them no more at all. The merchants of these things, made rich by her [Rome] **shall stand afar off for the fear of her torment, weeping and wailing, And saying, Alas, alas, that great city, that was clothed in fine linen, and purple, and scarlet, and decked with gold, and precious stones, and pearls! For in one hour so great riches is come to nought"** (18:14-17a).

Among the men and women of our day, a man may be a millionaire one day and the next day be almost a penniless pauper. A great city, a great state, a great nation may be highly affluent; people may have silver and gold, bank accounts, stocks and bonds, houses and lands, and in no time they may be swept away from them. James said that we know not what a day may bring forth.

"And every shipmaster, and all the company in ships, and sailors, and as many as trade by sea, stood afar off, And cried when they saw the smoke of her burning, saying, What *city is* **like unto this great city! And they cast dust on their heads, and cried, weeping and wailing, saying, Alas, alas, that great city, wherein were made rich all that had ships in the sea by reason of her costliness! for in one hour is she made desolate"** (18:17b-19).

This is the third time we read, "In one hour is she made desolate." It has taken centuries to build her, but in a very short time she is unbuilt.

"Rejoice over her, *thou* heaven, and *ye* holy apostles and prophets; for God hath avenged you on her" (18:20).

This is the judgment of the children of God. God has approved and judged Rome and the Roman Empire with His judgment.

"And a mighty angel took up a stone like a great millstone, and cast *it* into the sea, saying, Thus with violence shall that great city Babylon be thrown down, and shall be found no more at all. And the voice of harpers, and musicians, and of pipers, and trumpeters, shall be heard no more at all in thee; and no craftsman, of whatsoever craft *he be,* shall be found any more in thee; and the sound of a millstone shall be heard no more at all in thee; And the light of a candle shall shine no more at all in thee; and the voice of the bridegroom and of the bride shall be heard no more at all in thee: for thy merchants were the great men of the earth; for by thy sorceries were all nations deceived. And in her was found the blood of prophets, and of saints, and of all that were slain upon the earth" (18:21-24).

Edward Gibbon wrote his great study *The Rise and Fall of the Roman Empire.* These five volumes are a good commentary on the book of Revelation and the corruption of Rome. The scholarly German historian Theodor Mommsen has four volumes. The two volumes on the provinces of the Roman Empire bring out the same thing.

Revelation, particularly chapters 16 through 18, serve as a commentary on the condition of the Roman Empire. They emphasize the reality that it is tainted, that it is falling, and that the fall of it will be great and that it will not exist any more. It will be gone. It will be gone forever, but the church of the living God will continue to march triumphantly on, even after Rome has fallen.

CHAPTER 14

VICTORY

Revelation 19

This chapter presents the second coming of our Lord and the triumph of the church of the living God over the empire. We stated earlier in our study that the book of Revelation mirrors a great conflict, the conflict between God and the devil, between Christ and the Roman Caesars, between the empire and the church, between polytheism and monotheism, between truth and error, and between everything that is right and everything that was wrong. Keep in mind again the lines of Bryant's poem, "The Battlefield":

> Truth though crushed to earth shall rise again.
> The eternal years of God are hers.
> But error wounded writhes in pain
> And dies among his worshipers.

How abundantly true is that of Rome and her people.

"After these things," that is, the things of chapter 18, **"I heard a great voice of much people in heaven, saying, Alleluia; Salvation, and glory, and honour, and power, unto the Lord our God"** (19:1). They do not belong to the Roman Caesar, but they belong to our God.

"For true and righteous *are* his judgments" (19:2a). The judgments of Rome were unrighteous and untrue, but those of God are true and righteous.

"For he hath judged the great whore, which did corrupt the earth with her fornication, and hath avenged the blood of his servants at her hand" (19:2b). In Romans 12:19, Paul quoted from the Old Testament, saying, "It is written, Vengeance *is* mine; I will repay, saith the Lord." So here is the great harlot, Rome. She was the great adulteress who corrupted the earth. God judged her and avenged the blood of His servants. We've referred a number of times to the Christians being fed to the lions in the coliseum built during the reign of Vespasian and to the Christians burned at the stake in numerous places in the Roman Empire.

"And again they said, Alleluia. And her smoke rose up for ever and ever," that is, the smoke of Rome goes up, **"And the four and twenty elders and the four beasts fell down and worshiped God that sat on the throne, saying, Amen; Alleluia"** (19:3-4).

These 24 elders appeared first in chapter 4 where they appear to be representative of the heads of the 12 tribes of Israel and representative of the 12 apostles of the Lamb. The four living creatures (beasts) are representative of all creation. Together, the 24 elders and the four beasts joined in a great doxology that began with "amen," that is, "may it be so," and continued with "alleluia." The word "alleluia" literally means "praise." Psalm after psalm in the great book of Psalms begins with and continues with "alleluia."

"And a voice came out of the throne, saying, Praise our God." Don't give praise to the Caesars. Don't give praise to Rome, but give praise to our God **"all ye his servants, and ye that fear him, both small and great"** (19:5).

"And I heard as it were the voice of a great multitude, and as the voice of many waters, and as the voice of mighty thunderings, saying, Alleluia: for the Lord God omnipotent reigneth" (19:6). The Caesars don't reign. The kings in the Roman Empire don't reign, but the Lord God Omnipotent and Almighty reigns. He is in the saddle. He has not abdicated.

When Abraham Lincoln was assassinated, James A. Garfield, who was a preacher of the gospel and a general in the federal army during the Civil War, was in New York. All the people in New York and round about, all that knew about it, were very sad. They said, "Everything has come to an end! Lincoln has been killed." Garfield, speaking in a great park, said, "Remember the Lord God Almighty still reigns." That is the message of Revelation 18 and 19 and the whole book of Revelation — the triumphancy of the kingdom of God and the Lord Jesus Christ. We read in Hebrews 12:28, that we receive "a kingdom which cannot be moved." In Matthew 16:18, our Lord said, "The gates of Hades shall not prevail against it."

"Let us be glad and rejoice, and give honour to him," that is, unto God and Jesus Christ, **"for the marriage of the Lamb is come, and his wife hath made herself ready. And to her was granted that she should be arrayed in fine linen, clean and white: for the fine linen is the righteousness of saints"** (19:7-8).

In Ephesians 5 Paul compares the relationship between the members of the church and Jesus to the relationship between the bride and the groom. Paul, writing by the power of the Holy Spirit, said that the church, the bride of Christ, must be presented to Christ without spot, blemish or wrinkle. The church of the living God must present herself arrayed in fine linen of the righteous acts of the saints and be eternally present in the great marriage supper of the Lamb, presented without spot, blemish or wrinkle.

"And he saith unto me, Write, Blessed *are* they which are called unto the marriage supper of the Lamb. And he saith unto me, These are the true sayings of God. And I fell at his feet to worship him. And he said unto me, See *thou do it* not: I am thy fellowservant, and of thy brethren that have the testimony of Jesus: worship God: for the testimony of Jesus is the spirit of prophecy" (19:9-10).

In other words, the prophets of the Old Testament prophesied concerning the coming of the Lord Jesus Christ. Prophets beginning with Moses and concluding with Malachi placed a star upon the city of Bethlehem, where Jesus Christ was to be born, where wise men from afar would see His star and journey from the East to worship the One who was to be the new-born king of the Jews and of the world.

"And I [the apostle John on Patmos] **saw heaven opened, and behold a white horse; and he that sat upon him *was* called Faithful and True, and in righteousness he doth judge and make war"** (19:11).

The literal meaning here is that heaven was standing open, and John saw a white horse. White has always been emblematic of purity and of victory. It is none other than the Lord Jesus Christ himself seated upon the white horse. In Revelation 6:2, we read, "And I saw, and behold a white horse: and he that sat on him had a bow;

and a crown was given unto him: and he went forth conquering, and to conquer." Here the Lord Jesus is in the role of a great conqueror, not a military conqueror, but a spiritual conqueror. He is riding upon a white horse, which all who read or who heard this message would understand as a horse of victory and a horse of purity. "He that sat upon him *was* called Faithful and True." The Lord Jesus Christ is the One who is "Faithful and True." Others were unfaithful. He was true and others were untrue. He waged a war and judged in righteousness. War and judgment by the Romans were not in righteousness but in unrighteousness many times.

"His eyes *were* as a flame of fire" (19:12a), suggesting His omniscience, that He knows everything. All things are naked and laid open before His eyes. He knows what is in man. There is nothing hidden from Him. "On his head *were* many crowns" (19:12b). These crowns, or diadems, suggest royalty. "He had a name written, that no man knew, but he himself" (19:12c).

This reminds us of the promise to the overcomer, as addressed to the Pergamum Christians. "He that hath an ear, let him hear what the Spirit saith unto the churches; To him that overcometh will I give to eat of the hidden manna, and will give him a white stone, and in the stone a new name written, which no man knoweth saving he that receiveth *it*" (Revelation 2:17). In ancient times, as in all times, names had meaning. The idea that there is nothing in a name is totally untrue. Solomon said, "A *good* name *is* rather to be chosen than great riches" (Proverbs 22:1). Concerning the name of Jesus, Peter said, "Neither is there salvation in any other: for there is none other name under heaven given among men, whereby we must be saved" (Acts 4:12).

The Lord riding this white horse, conquering, "*was* clothed with a vesture dipped in blood" (this could be the blood of His enemies), "and his name is called The Word of God" (19:13). The first chapter of the gospel of John, written by the same author of Revelation, referred to our Lord as "the Word of God." The Greek word used here, *logos,* was a common word in the first century. The Gnostics and others used it. The Holy Spirit took it and fumigated it and baptized it, cleaned it, and put Christian meaning into it. So here reference is to our Lord as the Word of God. There are two words translated "word" upon the pages of the Greek New Testament.

They are *logos* and *ramah*. *Logos* has personality; *ramah* refers to the written or spoken word.

"And the armies *which were* in heaven followed him upon white horses, clothed in fine linen, white and clean" (19:14). We understand these armies metaphorically, not as we usually understand armies, but they were spiritual armies going forth to conquer.

"And out of his mouth goeth a sharp sword, that with it he should smite the nations: and he shall rule them with a rod of iron: and he treadeth the winepress of the fierceness and wrath of Almighty God" (19:15).

Now He has a sharp sword. "For the word of God *is* quick, and powerful, and sharper than any twoedged sword, piercing even to the dividing asunder of soul and spirit, and of the joints and marrow, and *is* a discerner of the thoughts and intents of the heart" (Hebrews 4:12). Part of the Christian soldier's uniform is "the sword of the Spirit, which is the word of God" (Ephesians 6:17). So the sword with which the commander-in-chief of the greatest army that ever marched in heaven or on earth takes is the sword of the Spirit with which He can divide joint and marrow, and with which He can conquer as He goes forth. Not only this, He is going to rule the nations with a rod of iron. This reminds us of the second psalm, which is a messianic psalm and said the Messiah would rule with a rod of iron.

"And he hath on *his* vesture and on his thigh a name written, KING OF KINGS, AND LORD OF LORDS" (19:16).

We had this earlier in chapter 11, where He is described as the King of kings and Lord of lords. The Christians of the seven churches were reminded on every hand that Domitian was King of kings and Lord of lords, and that before him Titus was and before Titus, Vespasian, the father of both Titus and Domitian. Other preceding Caesars thought of themselves as King of kings and Lord of lords. But God reminds the Christians of western Asia Minor that it is not the Caesars, but the Lord Jesus Christ who is King of kings and Lord of lords. Remember the beautiful "Hallelujah Chorus," which reaches one climax after another until at last they come to the climax of all climaxes with the singing of "King of kings and Lord of lords."

"And I saw an angel standing in the sun [figurative language] **and he cried with a loud voice, saying to all the fowls that fly in the midst of heaven, Come and gather yourselves together unto**

the supper of the great God; That ye may eat the flesh of kings, and the flesh of captains, and the flesh of mighty men, and the flesh of horses, and of them that sit on them, and the flesh of all *men, both* free and bond, both small and great" (19:17-18).

The Old Testament and extra-biblical literature often mention birds of prey. Here we have birds of prey coming down on men who are kings and captains and upon horses and other creations of God. Here in figurative language is a tremendous contrast between the great marriage supper of the Lamb for the children of God, and the fate of the so-called mighty men of the earth.

"And I saw the beast [the Roman emperor] and the kings of the earth [the kings of the provinces of the Roman Empire] And their armies, gathered together to make war against him that sat on the horse, and against his army. And the beast was taken, and with him the false prophet that wrought miracles before him, with which he deceived them that had received the mark of the beast, and them that worshiped his image. These both were cast alive into a lake of fire burning with brimstone. And the remnant were slain with the sword of him that sat upon the horse, which *sword* proceeded out of his mouth: and all the fowls were filled with their flesh" (19:19-21)

Here we meet the beast, the Roman emperor, and the false prophets who carried out the worship of the beast for the last time. The Lord casts them into the lake of fire. They are going to be annihilated, no more heard of, no more known, except as they shall burn in hell forever and forever and ever.

So we have here in Revelation 19 the great message of the reality of the victory of the Lord Jesus Christ and the church of the living God. In fact, any commentary written about Revelation, could be titled, *Victory!* That's what it is all about — victory for the cause of the Lord. My heavenly Father shall root up every plant that He hath not planted, but the Lord Himself has planted the church of the living God. "And in the days of these kings shall the God of heaven set up a kingdom, which shall never be destroyed: and the kingdom shall not be left to other people, *but* it shall break in pieces and consume all these kingdoms, and it shall stand for ever" (Daniel 2:44). Thank God for such great assurance of the triumphancy and the victory of the church of the living God.

CHAPTER 15

PREMILLENNIALISM

Revelation 20:1-10

When we come to Revelation 20, we come to what many consider the most difficult of all the chapters in the Bible. I would suggest, however, that it is one of the easiest chapters to understand, if you will study it through first-century glasses. It is easy to understand if we will sit where John sat when he wrote it, if we will sit with the members of the seven churches addressed in Revelation 1-3.

"And I saw an angel come down from heaven, having the key of the bottomless pit and a great chain in his hand" (20:1).

This is not the first time in Revelation that we have seen an angel coming down out of heaven, yet it is the first time that some build a whole doctrine around that angel coming down out of heaven. Some take this statement out of proportion and meaning and build up a mountain of doctrine.

An angel is a messenger of God. He comes with a commission from heaven. He is coming down out of heaven having the key of the bottomless pit or abyss. The abyss is the place occupied by those unprepared to meet God when they depart this life and by the devil and his angels. Not only did this angel have the key of the abyss, but he had a great chain in his hand. This chain is indicative of binding, of restricting, of confining. The first question we must ask is, Were the key and chain that this angel had literal? If they were literal, what kind of key and chain were they? Were they iron? Were they silver? Were they gold? Were they wood? Or just what kind? Clearly, it is a figure of speech. Scripture does not tell us what kind they were. That matters little. The message is that this angel had authority and that he had a means of using this authority. We cannot take it literally unless we take the rest of the chapter that way, which we cannot do.

"And he [the angel] **laid hold on the dragon, that old serpent, which is the Devil, and Satan, and bound him a thousand years"** (20:2). The dragon is identified as the old serpent, and in Genesis 3 we have the record of the devil coming to Eve in the form of a serpent. The old serpent is the devil. The word "devil" is a translation of the Greek word *diabolos. Dia* is a preposition that means "through," and *balo* means "to throw, or throw through." So the devil works to "throw through" and hurt others. He is also called "Satan," from the word *satanas.* In the book of Job, Satan came among the sons of God and was walking up and down in the land accusing people. God asked him if he had tried His servant Job. The devil's reply was that Job only served God because of what he could get out of him. So the devil accused Job of selfishness in serving the Lord. That is characteristic of his work.

This old serpent, the devil and Satan, was bound for a thousand years, and God **"cast him into the bottomless pit, and shut him up, and set a seal upon him, that he should deceive the nations no more, till the thousand years should be fulfilled: and after that he must be loosed a little season"** (20:3).

The pages of the Bible present the devil as the great deceiver. Paul tells in 2 Corinthians 11:4 that he can appear as an angel of light, so that he may appear as a friend to those whom he approaches. There are many other references to his deception. Paul referred to the fact that he deceived Eve. He is the ultimate deceiver. John tells that he was cast into an abyss and sealed until 1,000 years were finished. After this he must be loosed a little time. Are these thousand years a literal thousand years? If so, when did they begin, and when shall they end, or are they to begin and end at a certain time?

In the book of Enoch there is a reference to the binding of Satan 10,000 years. Of course Enoch is a non-canonical, uninspired book, but the New Testament refers to the fact that "one day *is* with the Lord as a thousand years, and a thousand years as one day" (2 Peter 3:8). The psalmist says, "A thousand years in thy sight *are but* as yesterday when it is past, and *as* a watch in the night" (Psalm 90:4).

Psalm 50:10 tells that "every beast of the forest *is* mine, *and* the cattle upon a thousand hills." Does this statement mean a literal thousand hills, or is it a way to express a very large number of hills, and a very large number of cattle that may be grazing upon those hills? Whatever a thousand years means, we find them mentioned six times in this chapter.

"And I saw thrones, and they sat upon them, and judgment was given unto them" (20:4a).

Concerning thrones, we remember Paul said, "Do ye not know that the saints shall judge the world?" (1 Corinthians 6:2). Our Lord told the apostles they would sit upon 12 thrones judging the 12 tribes of Israel (Matthew 19:28). Rome had for too long been in the saddle as the judge. Her judges throughout her vast domain sat upon many thrones judging the children of God, but now the tables are turned, things are reversed and the children of God are now sitting on thrones judging those who are not God's children. The children of God were the ones judged before, but now they are the judges.

"And *I saw* the souls of them that were beheaded for the witness of Jesus, and for the word of God, and which had not worshiped the beast, neither his image, neither had received *his* mark upon their foreheads, or in their hands, and they lived and reigned with Christ a thousand years" (20:4b).

There are those who teach that Revelation 20:4 refers to a future time when the children of God will reign for a literal thousand years upon this earth, judging the nations with Christ.

Read the text again, carefully and prayerfully. The "they" had been beheaded for the witness of Jesus and for the word of God and such that did not worship the beast (the Roman emperor) or his image and did not receive his mark (as required in chapter 13) on their foreheads or hands. "[A]nd they lived" and reigned with Christ a thousand years. Now that is just as plain as "He that believeth and is baptized shall be saved" (Mark 16:16). That statement is very simple, very understandable, but not any more understandable than this very clear, unclouded statement concerning those who *lived*. That verse is in the past tense. It was they who reigned, that is in the past tense, with Christ a thousand years. Isn't that plain? Who said the book of Revelation is hard to understand? It takes help *not* to understand it.

We read earlier, "And when he had opened the fifth seal, I saw under the altar the souls of them that were slain for the word of God, and for the testimony which they held: And they cried with a loud voice, saying, How long, O Lord, holy and true, dost thou not judge and avenge our blood on them that dwell on the earth? And white robes were given unto every one of them; and it was said unto them, that they should rest yet for a little season, until their fellowservants also and their brethren, that should be killed as they *were,* should be fulfilled" (Revelation 6:9-11). Revelation 20:4 is a fulfillment of the prayer made by these martyred souls John saw beneath the altar.

There are those who say that Revelation 20:1-4 teaches that when the Lord Jesus comes, that is, they teach with other scriptures that they marshal together to support this, only the dead in Christ will be raised. The dead outside of Christ will remain in their graves. The dead in Christ, along with the living in Christ, will be caught up in the clouds to meet the Lord in the air, and they, with the Lord, will have union in the sky. At the end the Lord, with the dead and the alive in Christ, will go to Jerusalem to be seated upon David's throne. The Mount of Olives will split wide open, two rivers running to the Dead Sea, and two rivers running to the Mediterranean. God will reestablish the old Jewish temple and reinaugurate the Jewish sacrifices. Christ will be on David's throne for a literal thousand years, with the devil bound for a literal thousand years.

This theory is premillennialism. The word "pre," of course, means "before," and "millennial" means a "thousand years." In this case, it means that the Lord will come before the millennium, before the thousand years of peace when the lion and the lamb shall lie down together and when little children shall play upon the holes of asps or snakes. Many people hold this theory.

John 5:28-29 says, "Marvel not at this: for the hour is coming, in the which all that are in the graves shall hear his voice, And shall come forth; they that have done good, unto the resurrection of life; and they that have done evil, unto the resurrection of damnation." There our Lord teaches definitely one resurrection of different kinds, different quality: a resurrection of the righteous and a resurrection of the unrighteous. These resurrections are virtually simultaneous. They are different in quality. This Scripture rules out a thousand years of reigning upon the earth with a separation of the resurrection of the unrighteous by one thousand years.

In addition, concerning premillennialism, the theory says that after the thousand years the Lord will raise the dead out of Christ and loose the devil, who will gather his armies, and the Lord will gather His armies, and they will meet on the plains of Megiddo. There they will fight the battle of Armageddon, which will wind up everything. That little plain could not remotely begin to hold one-millionth of the people who have lived from Adam's time and who shall live until the end of time. The battle of Armageddon is a spiritual battle fought upon the hearts of men and women concerning what is right and wrong.

Another argument against premillennialism is that nowhere does Scripture teach that there is going to be a glorious union of the Lord and His church up in the sky. Nowhere does Scripture teach that God intends to rebuild the old Jewish temple. If that is true, we might as well throw out the whole book of Hebrews. All of its teaching is against anything like the restitution of the old law and the reestablishment of the Jewish sacrifices. That concept is foreign to the New Testament from beginning to end.

As for the Mount of Olives being split open, that idea comes by taking Zechariah's words out of context. Proponents make a pretext out of Zechariah so that it will teach what it does not really teach. As for the premillennial idea of the devil being bound for a literal 1,000 years, that is also foreign to the rest of the Bible. What is being taught concerning the binding of Satan is this: the cause for which these Christian martyrs lived and died is triumphant. God's people conquer the devil and all of his forces. "Then *cometh* the end, when he shall have delivered up the kingdom to God, even the Father; when he shall have put down all rule and all authority and power. For he must reign, till he hath put all enemies under his feet. The last enemy *that* shall be destroyed *is* death" (1 Corinthians 15:24-26).

The "loosing for a little season" refers to certain times of persecution, such as those under Diocletian, Marcus Aurelius and Julian the Apostate, all pagan emperors. The devil is loosed through them just for a little season.

To repeat, the teachings of these first four verses are that Jesus Christ is triumphant over the Caesars; God is victorious over the devil; the church is victorious over the Roman Empire; monotheism is victorious over polytheism; right is victorious over wrong. In the end the church of the living God is triumphant over all forces, and every plant that God has not planted will certainly be rooted up.

"But the rest of the dead lived not again until the thousand years were finished. This *is* the first resurrection" (20:5).

The first resurrection is the resurrection of the triumphancy of the cause for which Christians lived and died, a cause that at times seemed to be defeated but is now come out on top, triumphant and victorious.

"Blessed and holy *is* he that hath part in the first resurrection: on such the second death hath no power, but they shall be priests of God and of Christ, and shall reign with him a thousand years" (20:6).

The thousand years indicate a long time in comparison with the short time the Christians suffered persecution. The thousand years is the time in which the children of God can count their triumphancy over the pagan powers of Rome.

The first resurrection does not apply to baptism. The resurrection out of the watery grave was first advocated by Augustine, one of the early theologians of the Catholic church. Others followed him, but it cannot refer to baptism because they who take part in the first resurrection have no part in the second death. In other words, if they are once saved, they will always be saved. If the first resurrection is baptism, it is impossible to apostatize. If you are once resurrected from the watery grave, the second death will have no power over you. As long as you live, regardless of what you do, all things will be right for you concerning the end of time. We know that the totality of the New Testament is against this.

CHAPTER 16

THE WORLD'S LAST DAY

Revelation 20:11-15

"Behold, he cometh with clouds; and every eye shall see him, and they *also* which pierced him: and all kindreds of the earth shall wail because of him. Even so, Amen" (Revelation 1:7).

"Heaven and earth shall pass away: but my words shall not pass away" (Mark 13:31).

"But the day of the Lord will come as a thief in the night; in the which the heavens shall pass away with a great noise, and the elements shall melt with fervent heat, the earth also and the works that are therein shall be burned up" (2 Peter 3:10).

"And the heaven departed as a scroll when it is rolled together; and every mountain and island were moved out of their places" (Revelation 6:14).

"And I saw a new heaven and a new earth: for the first heaven and the first earth were passed away; and there was no more sea. And I John saw the holy city, new Jerusalem, coming down from God out of heaven, prepared as a bride adorned for her husband. And I heard a great voice out of heaven saying, Behold, the tabernacle of God *is* with men, and he will dwell with them, and they shall be his people, and God himself shall be with them, *and be* their God. And God shall wipe away all tears from their eyes; and there shall be no more death, neither sorrow, nor crying, neither shall there be any more pain: for the former things are passed away" (Revelation 21:1-4).

Every man and woman who has lived since Adam and Eve, except those who are now living, has had a last day upon this earth.

He or she may have died in infancy, in childhood, in the bloom of youth, in middle life or in old age, but to each of them, the last day in this world has come. Every person living today knows that he will have a last day.

He may die a natural death in which loved ones will be around him speaking softly and endearingly and bidding him good-bye as his face fades in the twilight of time. He may die in an automobile or airplane crash or in some other unexpected way, but his last day will come!

Although one by one we are all going down the valley, the time is coming when this world will have its last day. People will experience time no more. Kings and queens on their thrones, governmental presidents in their chairs, legislators in their seats, governors in their offices, armies in their quarters or on their battlefields and ambassadors in other lands will witness the world's last day. Doctors with their patients, teachers in their classrooms, business and professional people in their offices, workers in factories, farmers in fields, ministers in their pulpits and mothers in their homes with children in their arms will witness the world's last day.

We know not when the world's last day will be, but we know definitely that there will be the last day for this world and all that is in it. In Southern Europe in the Middle Ages, there were those who believed the world was coming to an end in their lifetime. They sold all they had and dressed themselves in white, flowing garments for the end, but it did not come. Across the decades and centuries there have been many date setters for the world's last day, but all have missed it. Truly, only God knows when it will be. "But of that day and *that* hour knoweth no man, no, not the angels which are in heaven, neither the Son, but the Father" (Mark 13:32). That we do not know the time of the world's last day does not lessen its reality and certainty. Truly, this unknowable increases the importance of being ready for the world's last day. Whenever it comes, eternity will come into time and these realities will become experiences: the second coming of Christ, the general resurrection, the final judgment, hell and heaven.

Many passages underscore the reality of the second coming of Christ. "And while they looked stedfastly toward heaven as he went up, behold, two men stood by them in white apparel; Which also said, Ye men of Galilee, why stand ye gazing up into heaven? this same Jesus, which is taken up from you into heaven, shall so come in like manner as ye have seen him go into heaven" (Acts 1:10-11).

"Let not your heart be troubled: ye believe in God, believe also in me. In my Father's house are many mansions: if *it were* not *so,* I would have told you. I go to prepare a place for you. And if I go and prepare a place for you, I will come again, and receive you unto myself; that where I am, *there* ye may be also" (John 14:1-3).

"And as it is appointed unto men once to die, but after this the judgment: So Christ was once offered to bear the sins of many; and unto them that look for him shall he appear the second time without sin unto salvation" (Hebrews 9:27-28).

"Behold, he cometh with clouds; and every eye shall see him, and they *also* which pierced him: and all kindreds of the earth shall wail because of him. Even so, Amen" (Revelation 1:7).

How is He coming? He will come as He went. He "shall so come in like manner as ye have seen him go into heaven" (Acts 1:11). "Lift up your heads, O ye gates; and be ye lift up, ye everlasting doors; and the King of glory shall come in" (Psalm 24:7). "And Enoch also, the seventh from Adam, prophesied of these, saying, Behold, the Lord cometh with ten thousands of his saints" (Jude 14). "Every eye shall see him" (Revelation 1:7).

Why is He coming? He is coming to gather His own unto himself. "And to you who are troubled rest with us, when the Lord Jesus shall be revealed from heaven with his mighty angels, In flaming fire taking vengeance on them that know not God, and that obey not the gospel of our Lord Jesus Christ: Who shall be punished with everlasting destruction from the presence of the Lord, and from the glory of his power" (2 Thessalonians 1:7-9).

The words of John 5:28-29 demonstrate the certainty of the general resurrection: "Marvel not at this: for the hour is coming, in the which all that are in the graves shall hear his voice, And shall come forth; they that have done good, unto the resurrection of life; and they that have done evil, unto the resurrection of damnation." Paul said, "If in this life only we have hope in Christ, we are of all men most miserable" (1 Corinthians 15:19).

Paul understood our desire to know of the resurrection. "For we know that if our earthly house of *this* tabernacle were dissolved, we have a building of God, an house not made with hands, eternal in the heavens. For in this we groan, earnestly desiring to be clothed upon with our house which is from heaven" (2 Corinthians 5:1-2). He explained the nature of the resurrection by comparing the natural and the spiritual body: "It is sown in corruption; it is raised in incorruption: it is sown in dishonour; it is raised in glory: it is sown in weakness; it is raised in power: it is sown a natural body; it is raised a spiritual body" (1 Corinthians 15:42b-44a).

The "Why?" of the resurrection is explained by the fact that "flesh and blood cannot inherit the kingdom of God" (1 Corinthians 15:50).

The world's last day underscores the reality of the final judgment. The world's last day will witness the final assize of all time, when God will judge the uncounted teeming millions for all time and for all eternity. Not until "heaven and earth are passed away" will the judgment begin. There never has been and there never will be any other such a judgment. "For we must all appear before the judgment seat of Christ; that every one may receive the things *done* in *his* body, according to that he hath done, whether *it be* good or bad" (2 Corinthians 5:10). "And the times of this ignorance God winked at; but now commandeth all men every where to repent: because he hath appointed a day, in the which he will judge the world in righteousness by *that* man whom he hath ordained; *whereof* he hath given assurance unto all *men,* in that he hath raised him from the dead" (Acts 17:30-31).

John gives a graphic portrayal of the judgment: **"And I saw a great white throne, and him that sat on it, from whose face the earth and the heaven fled away; and there was found no place for them. And I saw the dead, small and great, stand before God; and the books were opened: and another book was opened, which is *the book* of life: and the dead were judged out of those things which were written in the books, according to their works. And the sea gave up the dead which were in it; and death and hell delivered up the dead which were in them: and they were judged every man according to their works"** (Revelation 20:11-13)

"And I saw a great white throne, and him that sat on it" (20:11a). It is great a great throne because it is God's. The thrones of the Roman emperors were nothing in comparison to the great throne of God. Their power was limited while God was and is all powerful. The emperors could be only one place at a time while God was so great that He could be everywhere. If one made his bed in Sheol or took wings of the morning and dwelt in the uttermost parts of the sea, God would be there (Psalm 139:8-10). The white throne is emblematic of the stainless purity of the God Who sits upon it. Its whiteness also indicates the clear light that will reveal all lives of men. Note there is only one throne, in contrast to the many thrones of Revelation 20:4. His throne is supreme, and He is the Supreme Judge. The Caesars will not be the judge. Preachers, elders and critics will not be the judge. God and Jesus as One will be the judge. "For the Father judgeth no man, but hath committed all judgment unto the Son" (John 5:22).

"From whose face the earth and the heaven fled away; and there was found no place for them" (20:11b).

That the heaven and the earth are not able to stand before Him implies the greatness and holiness of God. The brightness of His countenance dissolved the universe and annihilated the laws which governed it (Acts 17:30-31). Paul exhorted Timothy, "I charge *thee* therefore before God, and the Lord Jesus Christ, who shall judge the quick and the dead at his appearing and his kingdom" (2 Timothy 4:1).

"And I saw the dead, small and great, stand before God; and the books were opened ... And the sea gave up the dead which were in it; and death and hell delivered up the dead which were in them: and they were judged every man according to their works" (20:12-13).

The dead — great and small — all stand before God. The sea gave up her dead. Death and Hades gave up their dead. The oceans of the world and seven seas have been the graves of multiplied millions. In John's day, the wreck of ships was a common occurrence in Mediterranean lands.

Death and Hades gave up their dead. The uncounted billions of graves in every clime of all time will open for their occupants to stand before the great Judge of the universe. The mausoleums and the burial urns of the world will stand ajar for the souls of men and women to appear before God and Jesus in the final judgment.

Hades, or Sheol, its Hebrew counterpart, the unseen world, will give up its dead. All who have died from Adam until the last day of time will come forth for the last judgment.

The small and great, as men evaluate, will be there. God is no respecter of persons. We must all stand before the judgment seat of Christ. The multi-millionaire and the penniless pauper, the highly educated and the ignorant, the potentates of all time and the powerless of every clime, the man who has a good Christian home and the homeless wanderer, the saint and the sinner, the young and the old, the preacher and the elder, the song leader and the deacon will be at the judgment. Elijah and Jezebel, Isaiah and Ahaz, Cain and Abel, Jeremiah and Jehoiakim, Daniel and Belshazzar, Mattathias and Antiochus Epiphanes, Paul and Nero, John the apostle and Domitian, Polycarp and Trajan will be there, However separated all of these have been in time, they will be together at the judgment.

By what will they be judged? Not by a religious paper or by the creeds of men. John states it in these words: **"and the books were opened: and another book was opened, which is *the book* of life: and the dead were judged out of those things which were written in the books, according to their works"** (20:12b).

John names two kinds of books. The books that contain the records of the deeds of men are first mentioned. Daniel prophetically spoke of it in these words: "thousand thousands ministered unto him, and ten thousand times ten thousand stood before him: the judgment was set, and the books were opened" (Daniel 7:10). The idea in Daniel, Revelation and elsewhere is that God keeps a record of the deeds of all men. Every man is the author of his own story in life. God accurately records it in His book. Every man writes his own judgment and that which judges him. We may not want to meet it again, but we must meet it again. Every unkind word we say will meet us again. Every sin we commit will face us again. John Keble, in "The Effect of Example," has written these lines:

> The deeds we do, the words we say,
> Into still air they seem to fleet,
> We count them ever past;
> But they shall last,
> In the dread judgment they
> And we shall meet.

The book of life is the second book of judgment. **"And another book was opened, which is *the book* of life"** (20:12). The idea of the "book of life" occurs often in the Bible. Psalm 69:28 states: "Let them be blotted out of the book of the living, and not be written with the righteous." Paul referred to his fellow-workers "whose names are in the book of life" (Philippians 4:3). To the overcomer in the church in Sardis, Jesus promised: "I will not blot out his name out of the book of life, but I will confess his name before my Father, and before his angels" (Revelation 3:5).

The Apocalypse of Baruch foretold the day when "the books shall be opened in which are written the sins of all those who have sinned, and again also the treasuries in which the righteousness of all those who have been righteous in creation is gathered" (2 Baruch 24:1).

Verse 15 gives the final rewards and sentences for those judged: **"And whosoever was not found written in the book of life was cast into the lake of fire."** Jesus spoke of this, the greatest separation of all time and eternity in Matthew 25. "And these shall go away into everlasting punishment: but the righteous into life eternal" (Matthew 25:46).

Hell awaits the sinner. **"But the fearful, and unbelieving, and the abominable, and murderers, and whoremongers, and sorcerers, and idolaters, and all liars, shall have their part in the lake which burneth with fire and brimstone: which is the second death"** (Revelation 21:8).

Heaven, the home of the soul, awaits the saved. The souls of men, wherever and whenever they have lived, have longed for a life better than this one. Abraham looked for that city with foundations, realizing he had no continuing city here. Paul longed for that better place: "For I am in a strait betwixt two, having a desire to depart, and to be with Christ; which is far better" (Philippians 1:23). All the martyrs revealed in the book of Revelation died that they might live.

The finale of all the book of Revelation is in the last part of the 20th and all the 21st and 22nd chapters. They present the total climax. The book is unfinished without them. Special attention should be given to the powerful words of Revelation 21:1-7 and 22:1-5.

CHAPTER 17

HEAVEN, WILL WE KNOW EACH OTHER THERE?

Revelation 21-22

"**And I saw a new heaven and a new earth: for the first heaven and the first earth were passed away; and there was no more sea. And I John saw the holy city, new Jerusalem, coming down from God out of heaven, prepared as a bride adorned for her husband. And I heard a great voice out of heaven saying, Behold, the tabernacle of God *is* with men, and he will dwell with them, and they shall be his people, and God himself shall be with them, *and be* their God. And God shall wipe away all tears from their eyes; and there shall be no more death, neither sorrow, nor crying, neither shall there be any more pain: for the former things are passed away**" (21:1-4). God permitted John to see the world's last day, when the sky and the earth are no more and the dreaded sea has gone and to behold beyond time "a new heaven and a new earth." The Roman Empire and its capital Rome have gone. All the empires of men with their capitals have faded away.

The word "heaven"is inscribed on millions of tombstones around the world. It has been the topic of conversation times without number. It has been the last word on the lips of uncounted thousands of Christians as they exchanged earth for eternity. Topics change with the mood of the times, but heaven is a perennial topic. Normal-minded people never tire of talking about it, singing about it and listening to sermons about it. Men and women, boys and girls around the world treasure it beyond expression. We cannot even measure the greatness of the topic of heaven.

Alfred Lord Tennyson expressed his view of the next life in his poem "Crossing the Bar," which he insisted must always be the last work in any collection of his poems.

> Sunset and evening star,
>   And one clear call for me,
> And may there be no moaning of the bar,
>   When I put out to sea.
>
> But such a tide as moving seems asleep,
>   Too full for sound and foam,
> When that which drew from out of the boundless deep
>   Turns again home.
>
> Twilight and evening bell,
>   And after that the dark!
> And may there be no sadness of farewell,
>   When I embark;
>
> For tho' from out our bourne of time and place
>   The flood may bear me far,
> I hope to see my Pilot face to face
>   When I have crossed the bar.

Heaven is a place of security. There are many fine houses in the great cities of the world. Their owners planned with the utmost care and appointed with the finest of furniture, and protected with the finest security systems. But many of these fine homes sometimes burn to the ground. The security they offered is not permanent. Nothing that is earthly can provide security that is eternal. It is only in heaven itself. The Lord promises security in heaven. **"Blessed *are* they that do his commandments, that they may have right to the tree of life, and may enter in through the gates into the city. For without *are* dogs, and sorcerers, and whoremongers, and murderers, and idolaters, and whosoever loveth and maketh a lie"** (Revelation 22:14-15).

In the second place, heaven is a place of activity. In Revelation 22:3, John stated that "his servants shall serve him." There will be work to be done in heaven. The moving lines of Rudyard Kipling in his poem "L'Envoi" offer that idea:

When earth's last picture is painted,
  and the tubes are twisted and dried,
When the oldest colors have faded,
  and the youngest critic has died,
We shall rest and faith, we shall need it,—
  lie down for an aeon or two,
Till the Master of All Good Workmen
  shall set us to work anew!
. . . .
And no one shall work for money,
  and no one shall work for fame,
But each for the joy of the working,
  and each, in his separate star
Shall draw the Thing as he sees It
  for the God of Things as They are!

Heaven is also a place of incredible and indescribable *beauty*. In 1 Corinthians 2:9, Paul quoted Isaiah, saying, "As it is written, Eye hath not seen, nor ear heard, neither have entered into the heart of man, the things which God hath prepared for them that love him." Isaiah was primarily referring to the good things of the Christian dispensation. But you and I must certainly believe that he ultimately made reference to the good things that await the children of God in heaven. "Eye hath not seen, nor ear heard, neither have entered into the heart of man, the things which God hath prepared for them that love him."

You and I are sitting at the brink of the Grand Canyon. We see that chasm made by the Colorado River across the centuries and say, "The firmament showeth his handiwork"(Psalm 19:1), as the canyon looks up toward the firmament. We stand at the edge of Niagara Falls and look from the American and the Canadian sides. We see those great falls, and we think of that great Old Testament phrase, "[D]eep calleth unto deep" (Psalm 42:7). We look at the majestic Alps, erected so high that they seem to kiss the skies. We see the beautiful skies come down as if they were going to caress the mountains, and we marvel at the beauty of God's creation.

We could go on and on about the beauties of God's creation. We could stand together on any clear night and look up into the sky. We would see one star differing from another star in glory, presenting a scene of unsurpassed beauty. We could truly say with David of old, "The heavens declare the glory of God; and the firmament showeth his handiwork" (Psalm 19:1).

Some time ago there was born to a Christian couple a beautiful baby girl. After some weeks, her parents discovered that she seemed to have vision problems. The parents consulted an opthamologist in their section. He told them regretfully, with tears in his eyes, "Your little Mary is almost blind. She may never be able to see. It is possible, however, that when she is twelve years old an operation may be able to give her almost normal vision." You can imagine how the parents of little Mary felt and how they anxiously waited through those twelve years trying to prepare Mary for the day when she might see. The years came and went, and they arranged for the leading eye surgeon in Europe to do the surgery. Mary and her parents went to the hospital which overlooked the Alps. After the surgery, the attendants rolled Mary back to her room. After some days, the surgeon, the nurses and the father and mother gathered anxiously around Mary's bed. As they removed the bandages from her eyes, Mary looked out the window toward the majestic Alps. Turning toward her mother, with tears running down her cheeks, she said, "Oh, Mother, why didn't you tell me it is so beautiful in this world?" The mother fell into her arms and said, "Mary, I tried to tell you, but I just couldn't."

When the redeemed children of God get home to glory, walk down the transparently golden streets of heaven and go in and out the pearly gates as they swing ajar on hinges of gold, we'll say, "Brother John, why didn't you tell us it's so beautiful up here?" He'll say to us, "Little children, I tried to tell you in the 21st and 22nd chapters of the book of Revelation, but I just couldn't." "Eye hath not seen, nor ear heard, neither have entered into the heart of man, the things which God hath prepared for them that love him."

It has not even entered into the heart of man the good things that God has prepared for those who love Him. We have not even remotely considered it. We have not at all conceived it. They are beyond our conception. They are so beautiful, so wonderful, so great.

The question remains. In this land concerning which we are talking so briefly, will we know each other? History's pages record that as long as men and women have believed in a life beyond this, they have believed that they will know those whom they have known here in that land beyond time and earth.

In 2 Samuel 11 there is the story of the baby boy of David near death. David would not eat nor sleep, would not dress himself presentably to friends and others and mourned day after day, hoping that his little boy would get well. After some days, however, the little fellow died. David shaved and dressed and ate and visited. Some of his close friends said, "David, we don't understand. How is it that you've done this?" Do you know what David's reply was? "While the child was yet alive, I fasted and wept: for I said, Who can tell *whether* God will be gracious to me, that the child may live? But now he is dead, wherefore should I fast? can I bring him back again? I shall go to him, but he shall not return to me" (2 Samuel 12:22-23). "I shall go to him." Now if David expected anything, he must have expected to have known this little baby boy when he went to him on the other side.

Matthew 17:1-5 provides the record of the transfiguration of the Lord Jesus Christ. Peter, James and John, the three apostles closest to Him, were there. Moses and Elijah were present. Peter proposed to Jesus, "Lord, it is good for us to be here: if thou wilt, let us make here three tabernacles; one for thee, and one for Moses, and one for Elijah." Peter had some way of recognizing Moses and Elijah, He had never seen them in person, but he had read about them a thousand times and he had heard about them more than a thousand times. He knew who they were.

In Luke 16 is the story of the rich man and Lazarus, who both died. The rich man lifted up his eyes in Tartarus, that compartment of the Hadean world where the wicked endure punishment in that intermediate realm between earth and heaven and hell. The rich man lifted up his eyes, looked across the great gulf and saw father Abraham. In the bosom of father Abraham, he beheld Lazarus who had daily lain at his gate desiring to be fed, not with the leftovers from the rich man's table, but with the crumbs that might fall from it. The rich man, knowing and fully recognizing Lazarus, cried out of the deepest depths of unbelievable anguish, "Father Abraham, have mercy on me, and send Lazarus, that he may dip the tip of his finger in water, and cool my tongue; for I am tormented in this flame"

(Luke 16:24). Now if anyone ever knew anyone beyond time and in the intermediate state and the land beyond this one, certainly the rich man must have known Lazarus.

There are passages in 1 John that give encouragement to the belief that we shall know each other over there. The general teaching of both the Old and New Testaments is that we shall know each other over there. Now of just what that knowledge will consist we are not able to say. It is a knowledge of recognition.

The Lord gives His invitation to the beauties of heaven saying, **"I Jesus have sent mine angel to testify unto you these things in the churches. I am the root and the offspring of David, and the bright and morning star. And the Spirit and the bride say, Come. And let him that heareth say, Come. And let him that is athirst come. A whosoever will, let him take the water of life freely"** (22:16-17). That which was lost in Eden is regained in heaven. The saints of all ages unite in their worship around the throne of God.

The book closes with warnings against adding to or taking away from the book. **"For I testify unto every man that heareth the words of prophecy of this book, If any man shall add unto these things, God shall add unto him the plagues that are written in this book: And if any man shall take away from the words of the book of this prophecy, God shall take away his part out of the book of life, and out of the holy city, and from the things which are written in this book"** (22:18-19). Surely God will not forget the malicious twisting of the book of Revelation by so many would-be teachers.

"He which testifieth these things saith, Surely I come quickly. Amen. Even so, come, Lord Jesus" (22:20). The Lord gives a last reminder that His message was one of a day and to a day. John anxiously awaited the fulfillment of all he wrote.

We close with John's own benediction: **"The grace of our Lord Jesus Christ be with you all. Amen"** (22:21).

STUDY QUESTIONS

Introduction

1. How is the book of Revelation the finale of the Bible?

2. Why have so many churches neglected the study of Revelation?

3. What are the advantages of studying Revelation "through first-century glasses"?

4. How could the Romans consider Christians to be atheists?

5. Why was the battle between the Roman Empire and the church so difficult?

Chapter 1

1. What is the basic meaning of an apocalypse or a revelation?

2. In what sense is Revelation a book of prophecy?

3. Why were the seven churches of Revelation 1-3 chosen?

4. What is the significance of "things which must shortly come to pass" and "at hand"?

5. How did this message from the One "which is, and which was, and which is to come" (1:8) encourage the early Christians?

6. What do we know about John, the writer of Revelation?

7. What does it mean that John was "in the Spirit on the Lord's day"?

8. What is Nero's significance to the background of Revelation?

Chapter 2

1. How did the Lord commend the Christians at Ephesus?
2. Why was leaving its "first love" (2:4) so serious?
3. How could the Ephesians avoid the Lord's condemnation?
4. Who was Polycarp? What is his significance in the early church?
5. How were the Smyrnans rich while in poverty?
6. What special problems faced the Christians at Pergamum?
7. What were the sins of the Nicolaitans?
8. What blessings were promised if the Christians at Pergamum overcame?
9. How were the works of the Thyatirans different from those of the Ephesians?
10. Who was trying to seduce the Christians in Thyatira?

Chapter 3

1. Are there many churches today like the church at Sardis?
2. What advice did the Christians at Sardis receive?
3. What principles can we draw from the Lord's promise to the faithful at Sardis that He would not blot their names out of the Book of Life?
4. What distinction did the churches at Smyrna and Philadelphia share concerning condemnation?
5. What does the "open door" at Philadelphia indicate?
6. What special programs challenged the Christians at Philadelphia?
7. Why would the Lord prefer Laodicea to be either hot or cold?
8. What added to the Laodiceans' problems of being lukewarm?
9. How does Christ knock at the door of the human heart?

Chapter 4

1. Who sat on the 24 thrones around the throne of God?
2. What were the four beasts around the throne?

3. What was special about the book in the right hand of the One on the throne?
4. How many seals did the book have?
5. How does the Lion of the tribe of Judah appear?
6. What is the important theme revealed in Revelation 6:9-10?
7. Are the horses of Revelation 6 to be taken literally?

Chapter 5

1. What does "angel" mean?
2. What are the "four corners of the earth" (7:1)?
3. Who are the 144,000 (7:4-8)?
4. Who make up the "great multitude" (7:9)?
5. Did salvation come from Rome?

Chapter 6

1. What does silence in heaven indicate (8:1)?
2. Who are the seven angels with seven trumpets (8:1)?
3. What does destruction of a third part of the sun, moon and stars indicate (8:12)?
4. Why would locusts and scorpions be feared so much?
5. What army is suggested by the plague of locusts and scorpions?

Chapter 7

1. What is indicated by the saying "there should be time no longer" (10:6)?
2. What prophet had an experience with a little book similar to John?
3. What important war lasted 42 months?
4. Who are the two witnesses (11:3)?
5. How is Revelation 11:15 the key verse of Revelation?

Chapter 8

1. Who is the woman clothed with the sun, moon and a crown of 12 stars (12:1)?
2. How did the dragon attempt to devour the child (12:4)?
3. What does the casting down of Satan indicate?
4. What are other equivalents of 42 months?
5. When did Christians flee to the wilderness?

Chapter 9

1. Why did the Romans have such trouble with the Parthians?
2. What rumor developed about Nero's return?
3. How did the Roman priests deceive the people?
4. Why was having the mark of the beast important?
5. Who does 666 point to?

Chapter 10

1. Are the 144,000 of chapter 7 and those of chapter 14 the same group?
2. Why could only 144,000 learn the new song (14:3)?
3. What happened to those who worshiped the beast (14:9-10)?
4. Who are the "blessed dead" of Revelation 14:13?
5. What is the "winepress of the wrath of God"?
6. What is a doxology?

Chapter 11

1. Why would the pouring out of the vials of wrath encourage the early Christians?
2. What brought about Rome's destruction?
3. What was special about Armageddon?
4. Is the battle of Armageddon a physical battle?
5. Who are some who have fought the battle of Armageddon?

Chapter 12

1. What did "harlot" mean to the first-century Christians?
2. How are Babylon and Rome connected?
3. How was Rome identified by the seven mountains (17:9)?
4. Who is "Lord of lords, and King of kings" (14:14)?
5. Who first suggested that the woman in 17:18 was the Roman Catholic Church?

Chapter 13

1. Why was Babylon called the great Babylon?
2. What was the fornication of Babylon (18:3)?
3. What was one of Rome's worst sins according to Revelation 18:7?
4. Why was trade so important to Rome?
5. Why would the merchants cry at the desolation of Rome (18:17-19)?

Chapter 14

1. Can we be sure that truth will overcome?
2. What is the essential message of Revelation 18-19?
3. What is the "marriage supper of the Lamb" (19:9)?
4. Who was riding the white horse (19:11)?
5. What is the significance of the name on his vesture and thigh (19:16)?

Chapter 15

1. How can the study of Revelation 20 be made easier?
2. How are the words "devil," "Satan" and "dragon" related?
3. Who will reign for 1,000 years, according to Revelation 20:4?
4. What is premillenialism?
5. What is the first resurrection (20:5)?

Chapter 16

1. Who will have a "last day"?
2. Can we predict when the world's last day will be?
3. What are some facts we know about the Lord's second coming?
4. Who will be at the judgment?
5. By what will mankind be judged?
6. What is the Book of Life?'

Chapter 17

1. Why is "heaven" such a beautiful word?
2. What are some special qualities of heaven?
3. Can we really understand how beautiful heaven is while we live?
4. Will we know each other in heaven?
5. What are some biblical passages that support the view that we will know each other in heaven?